DESERTER

DESERTER

BUSH'S WAR ON MILITARY FAMILIES, VETERANS, AND HIS PAST

IAN WILLIAMS

NATION BOOKS
NEW YORK

DESERTER:
Bush's War on Military Families, Veterans, and his Past

Published by
Nation Books
An Imprint of Avalon Publishing Group
245 West 17th St., 11th Floor
New York, NY 10011

AVALON
publishing group incorporated

Library of Congress Cataloging-in-Publication Data is available.

ISBN 1-56025-627-3

9 8 7 6 5 4 3 2 1

Book design by Maria Elias

Printed in the United States of America
Distributed by Publishers Group West

Personally, to Anora Mahmudova and our son Ian Anton Norbek Williams, who at four months old puzzled at paternal attention deprivation while we turned this book around.

Professionally, to Carl Bromley, Ruth Baldwin, Mike O'Connor, and Josh Buzzell from Nation Books, who helped turn it around so quickly in the hope that it would make a difference and to all the dedicated amateur and professional researchers into the memory hole of Bush's career, whose work I mined for this book.

And above all, for all those, American, Iraqi, British, Vietnamese, and others who have died in unnecessary wars that George W. Bush has supported or instigated. May there be an end to them soon.

TABLE OF CONTENTS

TIMELINE

GEORGE W. BUSH
June 12, 1942
Bush Sr. leaves Andover, joins the navy.

THE REAL WORLD
Bush Sr.'s father trading with Nazis.

GEORGE W. BUSH
September 2, 1944
Bush Sr.'s plane shot down.

GEORGE W. BUSH
July 6, 1945
George W. Bush born in New Haven, Conn.

GEORGE W. BUSH
Spring 1948
The Bush clan moves to Texas.

GEORGE W. BUSH
1958
Bush Sr. does Houston. Takes family.

THE REAL WORLD
1963
Dick Cheney gets first of four student deferments for draft. He later told the *Washington Post* he had "other priorities."

GEORGE W. BUSH
1964
Bush Jr. leaves Andover. Goes to Yale, on a hereditary affirmative action program.

GEORGE W. BUSH
Works on Dad's failed senate campaign.

January 1966 to October 1968

GEORGE W. BUSH December 1966: Bush Jr. arrested for stealing Christmas wreath.

THE REAL WORLD 1966: USAF drops 600,000 tons of bombs on Vietnam.

THE REAL WORLD Bush Sr. becomes congressman.

THE REAL WORLD Cheney gets a marriage deferment.

THE REAL WORLD John Kerry graduates from Yale and volunteers for the navy.

December 25, 1967

GEORGE W. BUSH Bush "makes inquiries" about the National Guard over Christmas vacation.

THE REAL WORLD Kerry goes for five-month tour as ensign on frigate USS *Gridley* off Vietnam.

January 19, 1968

GEORGE W. BUSH Bush takes medical and aptitude test in Massachusetts. Fails medical, and scores 25 percent on his pilot aptitude test.

January to May 1968

GEORGE W. BUSH Speaker of the House in Texas at a request of a long-time Bush family friend, Sidney Adger of Houston, contacts the head of the Texas Air National Guard, Brig. Gen. James Rose, to get Bush in.

THE REAL WORLD LBJ announces he won't run in next election. Eugene McCarthy set to secure democratic nomination on anti-war platform.

January 30, 1968

THE REAL WORLD Tet Offensive begins in Vietnam.

GEORGE W. BUSH
February 21, 1968
Attends dental exam—fails.

GEORGE W. BUSH
March 7, 1968
Has one tooth pulled and another filled to render him fit to be a pilot.

THE REAL WORLD
March 16, 1968
Hundreds killed in My Lai Massacre.

THE REAL WORLD
March 1968
Pentagon requests 206,000 more troops for Vietnam.

THE REAL WORLD
May 1968
Pentagon calls up 24,500 reserves for Vietnam.

THE REAL WORLD Paris Peace Talks begin.

GEORGE W. BUSH
May 27, 1968
Bush applies to Texas Air National Guard and is accepted immediately despite 500 applicants for four slots.

GEORGE W. BUSH Checked "do not volunteer" for overseas assignment.

GEORGE W. BUSH Listed his "background qualifications" as "none."

GEORGE W. BUSH Signs that he wants to make "flying a lifetime pursuit." He also signs, "I understand that I may be ordered to active duty for a period not to exceed 24 months for unsatisfactory participation."

THE REAL WORLD Over 100,000 on waiting list for the National Guard.

GEORGE W. BUSH
May 28, 1968
Does it all again for the cameras.

June 9, 1968

GEORGE W. BUSH   Bush graduates from Yale—would have become eligible for draft.

THE REAL WORLD   Half a million U.S. forces in Vietnam, dying at 350 per week.

THE REAL WORLD   Robert Kennedy assassinated this month.

THE REAL WORLD   Kerry becomes lieutenant in U.S. Navy.

July 12, 1968

GEORGE W. BUSH   Federal Recognition Examining Board (made up of Texas ANG officers) reports Bush is qualified for promotion to second lieutenant in the 111th Fighter Interceptor Squadron.

July 14 to August 25, 1968

GEORGE W. BUSH   Bush does basic training in San Antonio.

THE REAL WORLD   Riots at Chicago Democratic Convention.

August 25, 1968

GEORGE W. BUSH   Made second lieutenant without the bother of going to OTC, having a pilot's license, or getting a decent test score.

September to November 1968

GEORGE W. BUSH   Goes on inactive duty status so he can campaign in Florida for Edward Gurney, playing the race card to win.

THE REAL WORLD   Richard M. Nixon elected president.

November 17

THE REAL WORLD   Kerry begins second tour in Vietnam as commander on Swift Boat 44.

November 26, 1968 and following year

GEORGE W. BUSH   Attends undergraduate pilot training with the 3559th Student Squadron, Moody Air Force Base, GA.

GEORGE W. BUSH   Nixon sends plane to take W. for a date with daughter Tricia.

THE REAL WORLD   Draft makes up 38 percent of U.S. forces in Vietnam—12 percent of draftees are students.

THE REAL WORLD   526,000 American troops in Vietnam.

December 2, 1968

THE REAL WORLD   Kerry wins first Purple Heart.

February to March 1968

THE REAL WORLD   Kerry wins second Purple Heart, Silver Star, and Bronze Star.

December 1969

GEORGE W. BUSH   Bush's guard service exempts him from lottery.

THE REAL WORLD   Bill Clinton writes his famous letter to Col. Holmes and puts himself forward for draft.

THE REAL WORLD   First lottery for draft since 1942. Clinton gets lucky number.

THE REAL WORLD   John Kerry voluntarily extends his term of office until August.

1970

THE REAL WORLD   Kerry asks for discharge to fight Congress seat. Leaves service with three Purple Hearts, a Bronze Star, and a Silver Star.

| | *May 15, 1970* |
| THE REAL WORLD | Four students protesting the war killed by National Guard at Kent State University. |

	June 23, 1970
GEORGE W. BUSH	Bush allegedly "explored" joining the Palace Alert program for overseas service, just before leaving combat training school.
THE REAL WORLD	This month Kerry joins Vietnam Veterans Against the War.

| | *June 30, 1970* |
| THE REAL WORLD | Palace Alert program wound up. |

	Fall 1970
GEORGE W. BUSH	Bush applies to University of Texas Law School. Is rejected.
THE REAL WORLD	Moratorium Day, October 15, brings millions to the streets against the war.

	November 1970
THE REAL WORLD	Bush Sr. loses Senate election to Lloyd Bentsen.
THE REAL WORLD	Kerry quits VVAW.

	January 1971
GEORGE W. BUSH	Bush assigned flying duty as a pilot of F-102 fighter interceptors, 111th Squadron at Ellington.
GEORGE W. BUSH	*Houston Post* mentions Bush Jr. considering a run for state senate position.
THE REAL WORLD	Bush Sr. becomes U.S. ambassador to UN.

June 13, 1971

THE REAL WORLD   The *New York Times* publishes Pentagon Papers establishing excuse for Vietnam War was fictitious.

August 24, 1971

GEORGE W. BUSH   Bush recommended for promotion to first lieutenant.

April 1, 1971

THE REAL WORLD   Congress passes two-year extension of draft, abolishes college exemption for freshmen.

April 16 , 1972

GEORGE W. BUSH   Bush takes last flight as a National Guard member.

THE REAL WORLD   Air Force introduces substance abuse tests for medicals.

May 15, 1972

GEORGE W. BUSH   Bush leaves his Texas unit and heads for Alabama.

May 24, 1972

GEORGE W. BUSH   Bush seeks a transfer from his Houston Guard unit to the 9921st Air Reserve Squadron a postal unit, in Montgomery, Ala., for an unpaid assignment while he campaigns for Red Blount, a friend of his father. The transfer is approved by the unit's commander. There is no record Bush reported for duty.

June to September 1972

GEORGE W. BUSH   Lt. Col. Calhoun, the only person who claims to have seen Bush in the Alabama National Guard testifies that he did drill at Dannelly in this period. Bush was not posted there until September.

July 6, 1972

GEORGE W. BUSH   Misses or fails (?) annual flight physical. Loses wings.

GEORGE W. BUSH

July 31, 1972
The Air Force Reserve Personnel Center overrules the May transfer request and returns Bush's application as "ineligible for assignment in the Air Reserve Squadron."

GEORGE W. BUSH

August 19 to 24, 1972
Bush Jr. goes with dad to Republican National Convention in Miami.

THE REAL WORLD Bush Sr. becomes RNC chair.

GEORGE W. BUSH

September 5, 1972
Air Force records revocation of Bush's flight status as of August 1 because of a "failure to accomplish annual medical examination."

GEORGE W. BUSH

September 6, 1972
Bush's request for a transfer to perform "equivalent duty" for the 187th TAC Recon Group based in Montgomery, Ala., is approved.

GEORGE W. BUSH

September 15, 1972
The Alabama Guard accepts Bush and directs him to report to Lt. Col. William Turnipseed. Turnipseed says he never met Bush.

GEORGE W. BUSH

September 29, 1972
Is suspended as a pilot for failure to take annual physical and ordered to present himself for a board. He doesn't. There is no record of his attendance.

GEORGE W. BUSH

December 1972
Supposedly returns to Texas. Supposedly meets John White and asked to work at PULL. Definitely in D.C. to offer his father a fistfight after drunken driving.

January to September 1973

GEORGE W. BUSH   Supposedly working full time at PULL. In 2004, Scott
                 McLellan evades the question of whether this was some
                 form of mandated community service. J.H. Hatfield
                 alleges Karl Rove is one of three sources confirming a
                 cocaine possession rap and community service.

THE REAL WORLD   January 28: Mission accomplished. Vietnam War ends
                 with no involvement by George W. Bush.

THE REAL WORLD   Vietnam ceasefire. Last U.S. troops brought home.

THE REAL WORLD   End of Draft.

January 6, 1973

GEORGE W. BUSH   W goes to the National Guard dentist in Alabama—
                 but not the flight medical. The only documented
                 appearance in the state!

May 2, 1973

GEORGE W. BUSH   His friend and commander says that they have not seen
                 him so cannot submit evaluation: "Lt. Bush has not
                 been observed at this unit during the period of report.
                 A civilian occupation made it necessary for him to
                 move to Montgomery, Alabama."

June 1973

GEORGE W. BUSH   The evaluation is returned to the Texas National
                 Guard with request for form 77a so "this officer can be
                 rated in the position he held."

May to July 1973

GEORGE W. BUSH   Bush is booked for thirty-six days of duty, but there are
                 no pay records, and he does not recall what he did. But
                 it did not involve flying.

	September 18, 1973
GEORGE W. BUSH	Applies for early discharge to go to Harvard Business School.

	October 1, 1973
GEORGE W. BUSH	Gets honorable discharge from National Guard, assigned to inactive reserve in Massachusetts.

	November 12, 1973
GEORGE W. BUSH	Texas National Guard's personnel office sends form 77a and says simply: "Not rated for the period 1 May 1972 through 30 Apr 73. Report for this period not available for administrative reasons."

	1974
GEORGE W. BUSH	The date after which George W. Bush is prepared to deny that he used illegal drugs.
THE REAL WORLD	September: Bush Sr. goes to China as ambassador.

	November 1974
GEORGE W. BUSH	Final inactive reserve discharge with honors—six months late, which some suggest may be a penalty added because of AWOL or other disciplinary action.

After graduating from Yale University in 1966, John Kerry volunteered for the navy and served two tours of duty in Vietnam. In his first tour, he spent four months on the USS *Gridley* frigate off Vietnam's shore. He volunteered for the second tour, where he served nearly five months as a swift boat commander in the Mekong Delta and won three Purple Hearts, a Bronze Star, and a Silver Star.

Kerry's three war injuries—all minor—were enough to allow him an early return to stateside duty. Kerry would have been discharged in December 1969 had he not voluntarily extended his tour of duty through the following August. But Kerry asked for an early release so he could run for Congress and was discharged in January 1970. Kerry then ran for a House seat in Massachusetts, but later gave up his bid for the democratic nomination. He joined Vietnam Veterans Against the War and became its leading spokesman. During a protest in April 1971, Kerry threw his war ribbons over a fence at the Capitol.

1 WHY BEAT THE BUSH?

WHEN INVITED TO WRITE a book about George W. Bush's military career, I thought that at least this would be mercifully short book: indeed a blank notebook, something of a joke, not least since the original deadline was April 1, April Fool's Day.

Then I remembered Laurence Sterne's classic shaggy-dog story, *The Life and Opinions of Tristram Shandy,* which ends its hundreds of pages on the day of its hero's birth, which could provide a model for the Bush "wag the dog" tale. I also realized that all over the world, scholars working on quantum physics and cosmology were, in fact, working very hard on the nature of nothing. The book commission forced me to become a thamnologist[1]—an expert on Bushes and shrubs—and I began to appreciate that the very absence of a genuine, hands-on, military career for Bush the Younger may well be one of the forces currently driving us all toward Armageddon.

From one way of looking at it, all over the world, men and women are now dying and being maimed because George W. Bush had lived through "the war of his generation," not only without firing a shot in anger, but also without being within a hemisphere of any such shot. In addition, the world's number one superpower is within a Chinese whisper of bankruptcy because a spoilt Ivy League jock is still trying to prove himself to his war-hero father and his roughneck Texas buddies. Bush the Elder was a genuine volunteer and war hero: he even had the temerity to denounce Ronald Reagan's "voodoo economics." Bush the Younger dodged the war and has given his country a genuinely Haitian-sized trade and budget deficit.

On the other hand, it may have little to do with Freud; in fact, Bush's military career has more to do with fraud. Many of George W. Bush's opponents, not least Saddam Hussein, but also many on the Liberal wing of American politics, will have realized by now that they grievously underestimated the president. They were quite right that he was, and still is, no intellectual, and certainly no philosopher-prince—but they did not recognize the hard core that made him a prince indeed, in the manner that Machiavelli described.

To get the same combination of lightweight intellect and ruthless appreciation of power, we have to return, as so often in this administration, to Lewis Carroll, who seems to have anticipated it all. George W. Bush's philosophy is modeled on Carroll's character Humpty Dumpty who cogently said, "The question is, which is to be master—that's all."

George W. Bush has been relentless in providing an answer to this question, and in pursuit of it, he has adopted

another Carrollist saying: "What I tell you three times must
be true." Above all this has applied to his supposed appreciation for and connection with the U.S. Armed Forces and his
continued pretensions of shared military experience.

For a mixture of personal, psychological, and sociological
reasons, and expedient political perceptions, all of which we
will address, George W. Bush has, even more since the 2000
election than before, wrapped himself in the flag. He continually refers to himself as "commander in chief," and dresses
up, whenever he can in quasi-uniform, and indeed he seems
to much prefer speaking to handpicked military audiences on
bases to addressing the unruly citizenry outside.

It is a continuation of the same role he used to have at
his Andover prep school—cheerleader for the football team,
where his job was to wear funny costumes and lead an
appreciative crowd in shared chanting. More sinisterly, one
has to look to Fidel Castro, or Saddam Hussein, to see
someone with a similar appreciation for military tailoring
and martial backdrops.

In looking at this important but elusive military career of
George W. Bush, you are reminded of his statement in the
autohagiography he published before the 2000 presidential
election about the important things in life, which he identi-
fied as "faith, family, and friends," to which he returned in
one of his first 2004 TV campaign ads. But you cannot help
adding, "fudging, fibbing, and falsification," as three allitera-
tive and essential tools he and his faithful friends and family
have constantly used to promote him—and presumably their
own interests. Typically, of course, Karen Hughes, his then

press secretary, actually wrote his autobiography, not Bush himself, whose first English grade at Andover was a zero.

Memory, or the lack of it, is as constant a thread as all those *f*'s in the Bush career. Most recently, he "could not recollect," a meeting with his counterterrorism advisors in the White House Situation Room, the day after the September 11 attack. Fortunately for posterity, Richard A. Clarke could, and fortunately for the White House's credibility, getting close to perjury on the issue, Condoleezza Rice eventually recalled it as well—although in somewhat different terms.

Similarly, his military record with the Texas Air National Guard, and his explanations of it, are orbited by recollections and nonrecollections that he and his team subject to constant revision as documentary evidence surfaces that spurs his cortex into more intense cerebration.

A dose of documentation has often cured his expedient amnesia. But then, so often, the documentation itself has developed some form of amnesia. The records of drills, attendances, and crucial correspondence all seem to have fallen down some memory hole in Texas or Alabama. Their absence is a continual accomplice to the intermittent attempts to put truth in the rumors his campaign spreads about his military service.

So why should it matter? After all, it was in another country, and besides, the war is over. On the face of it, it would be starkest hypocrisy for people like me and my colleagues at the *Nation* to complain about someone dodging the Vietnam draft. Those of us who were eligible for selective service also tried to avoid going to fight in a war we opposed and encouraged others to do the same. Those of us in other

countries demonstrated outside American embassies and con-
sulates and pressed our own governments not to follow
Lyndon Baines Johnson into the maelstrom.

We could even forgive the normal human frailties of
someone trapped by dynastic obligations into supporting the
Vietnam War and working for candidates who also did, yet
who used those same obligating connections to avoid the
messy fighting thing. If Bush had become a football player, a
rock star, or even a banker, his military career would have
sunk into the obscurity it so richly deserved.

But when that scion of a moneyed and privileged family,
whose main qualification has always been his inspired choice
of father and family, then runs for president on issues of
"character," and struts in borrowed military plumage on the
world stage while launching a real war that has killed thousands of real people, then he becomes fair game. In this work,
we seek to show just how spurious that martial plumage is
and just how insidiously he has appealed to military traditions
that he has no claim to. And indeed how dangerous for
democracy his caudillo-like appeal is.

One does not have to be a fan of President Bill Clinton to
wonder why his alleged draft dodging—which after all culminated in his putting his name in for the draft even if he had
the perennial Clintonesque luck in the draw—should be such
common currency on the airwaves, while there are people all
over the United States who will swear that George W. Bush
"served" in the military.

So, it seems proper, since the president has misappropriated
a soldierly mien, to look at his actual record: in the military

while he was in the National Guard, as a commander in chief in his conduct of the military policy of the United States, and, finally, to test him by the standards of all great commanders: *how he has looked after the welfare and safety of the troops whose command he has assumed.*

Although this book was written in haste, luckily we were able to draw upon the hard work of many intrepid journalists and concerned individuals who have plowed this field over and over again in a neo-Proustian attempt to rediscover memories of the presidential times that have been lost. It would be good, but entirely untrue, to say that we could draw upon the work of the alleged newspaper of record, the *New York Times*, to rebut this perception of Bush's service. However, for whatever reasons of deference or professional pique that lesser journals so often scooped them on this story, the *Times* did not seek to plow this field in any depth. The *Washington Post*, the *Boston Globe*, the *Dallas Morning News*, *Salon*, the *Texas Observer*, and many others have looked hard and fruitfully.

American voters, and the many people in the rest of the world who wish they had a ballot to cast against the most unpopular American president in world history, owe these reporters deep gratitude for their work and temerity in overcoming the traditional American media deference to those in authority. If the president wants to make his "character" the test for his reelection, while slandering his opponents, then it is good and meet that his own record be examined minutely—where it survives and can be examined.

2 TWELVE INCHES OF POWER: BUSH AND THRUST

KB TOYS ELITE FORCE AVIATOR:
GEORGE W. BUSH—U.S. PRESIDENT
AND NAVAL AVIATOR

ON A BRIGHT AND clear afternoon on May 1, 2003, the USS *Abraham Lincoln* cruised an hour's sailing offshore from San Diego, California, with many of its six thousand crew marshaled on its four-and-half acre deck. The carrier was returning after a ten-month assignment backing up "Operation Iraqi Freedom" in the Gulf, and before then supporting the war in Afghanistan. Over a thousand feet long, over twenty thousand tons deadweight, with two nuclear reactors humming along below decks, this, one of the biggest ships in the world's biggest navy, was a war groupie's ultimate wet dream.

With a roar, a Navy S-3B Viking shot past, not once, but twice, and then finally circled around to land on the carrier's flight deck, snagging the wires that stopped the plane and its participants from tumbling into the cold Pacific Ocean. The nominal copilot had actually been prepared for just that watery contingency; in the White House swimming pool, since the Viking's precious cargo was none other than President George W. Bush. As the plane snapped to a halt, the assembled crew, and the peak-time cable TV viewers, could see that "Navy 1" was emblazoned on the body of the aircraft and that just below the copilot's cockpit window, assiduous Navy sign painters had stenciled "George W. Bush commander in chief."

With the risible visual fate of former Democratic contender Michael Dukakis in mind, the president carefully removed his white flight helmet so the cameras could not catch him, Snoopylike, doing Red Baron imitations, before climbing down to the deck of the carrier. In his chic olive-colored flight suit, shod in combat boots, looking every inch the warrior, with the doffed helmet tucked under one arm, he raised his other in salute to the cheers of the sailors, who were lined under a huge banner declaring, "Mission Accomplished."

The historically minded may have noted that the ejection gear crossing his crotch bore more than a passing resemblance to a medieval codpiece. The effect of exaggerated masculinity and the enforced strutting gait was doubtless a serendipitous but welcome side effect.

Before he set off to the carrier, the president had already proclaimed May 1, "Loyalty Day," 2003. This had begun as an attempt to preempt worldwide socialism by expropriating May Day from disloyal and un-American types. First launched as "Americanization Day," not long after the Russian Revolution, all presidents since Eisenhower have proclaimed it in its present form as "Loyalty Day." But while presidents before may have been a little tongue-in-cheek, putting it on an implied par with Groundhog Day and similar routines in the calendar, this one was serious.

"Loyalty" is always a dubiously double-edged virtue, and surely un-American in that the country owes its origins to a profound act of disloyalty to a previous George, the Third, who had been the prince they toasted when he was rescuing the colonies from the French and the Indians a decade or so before. As Mark Twain qualified it, "Loyalty to the country always. Loyalty to the government when it deserves it."

One suspects that that such qualifications and niceties had been missing in the thoughts and speeches of the framers of the U.S. Patriot Act. However, Bush's proclamation came from the presidential heart, albeit perhaps via Karl Rove, who, rumor has it, may not actually have one of his own: "Today, America's men and women in uniform are protecting our nation, defending the peace of the world, and advancing the cause of liberty. The world has seen again the fine character of our nation through our military as they fought to protect the innocent and liberate the oppressed in Operation Iraqi Freedom."

In the old days in Moscow, May Day was the occasion for massive parades of Soviet might in front of the civilian Communist Party leadership. But this time Texan ingenuity and flamboyance reversed the roles. The American civilian leadership of the Republican Party was putting on a show for the U.S. military, assembled to watch from the observation deck.

In many ways, it *was* an iconic event, even if not for the same reasons that Fox TV declared it a "historic" event—headlining "commander in chief lands on USS *Lincoln*," Fox went on to report, "'Yes, I flew it. Yeah, of course, I liked it,' said Bush, who was an F-102 fighter pilot in the Texas Air National Guard after graduating from Yale University in 1968." It symbolized the Bush dynasty's second presidency in so many ways in its deafening sounds of silence, the suppression of inexpedient facts, and the elevation of dissimulative trifles.

For example, they forbore to mention that the four-seater Viking contained two real pilots and a Secret Service agent as well as the presidential pretender to pilothood. But we have to believe it because KB Toys almost immediately announced their twelve-inch "authentic military figure" of Elite Force Aviator: George W. Bush—U.S. President and Naval Aviator, showing the president in full Navy rig, looking thinlipped and tough-chinned from the package. Needless to say, neither Fox nor KB Toys tried to clutter the minds of their consumers with the controversies surrounding the president's early aviation career, let alone the constitutional niceties of an elected civilian leader with such a dangerous penchant for cross-dressing into military garb.

The commander in chief then wiled away the hours until peak TV news time pressing the flesh and celebrating the shared bonds of martial comradeship together with the sailors under his nominal command as, in the words of the *Wall Street Journal*, "he strutted" about the deck of the *Lincoln*.

When he eventually made his prime-time speech—the light from the setting sun, the "magic-hour" light, giving him a golden glow with highlighting shadows and the sea breeze tossing his locks—he announced the end of major hostilities. "Your courage—your willingness to face danger for your country and for each other—made this day possible," he told the crew, fully conscious that the cable-viewers of the world were hanging on to every word. He added, "When I look at the members of the United States military, I see the best of our country, and I am honored to be your commander in chief."

In fact, he often uses this title, just as he often dons military uniforms, which historically should be more disturbing to many Americans than it seems to be. It is not a costume that hangs well on elected civilian leaders. Abraham Lincoln, the *serious* war president who gave his name to the floating stage for the presidential performance, was never depicted in uniform, even though his militia men in the Black Hawk War had actually elected him captain, unlike Bush, breveted lieutenant because of his family's influence.

In fact, Lincoln complimented Oliver Wendell Holmes, then a serving captain, for calling him a "fool" when the president's stovepipe hat provoked a fusillade from the Confederate trenches as he peeked over during a visit to the Union front line. "I'm glad to see you know how to talk to a civilian," he told Holmes indulgently. As we shall see, no one has seen George W. Bush anywhere that close to the enemy— even though he does try to surround himself with a warrior-like penumbra.

If George W. Bush were just a little boy who had never really grown up, we could afford to be indulgent. Atavistic as it may, we primates do like marching to drums and brandishing weapons. Some of us overcome these primal instincts, others don't, but little boys will play soldiers even in pacifist families. As the late and lamented Peter Ustinov said, "At the age of four with paper hats and wooden swords, we're all generals. Only some of us never grow out of it."[2]

However, while there is certainly an immature jockish element to the president, there is a more sinister side to his dressing up games. By posing as the commander in chief in the "war on terror," with the aid of a media that is deferential to the point of obsequiousness, he has gone a long way to outlaw critical thinking, let alone criticism of both the targets and the methods of his war. For many Americans, criticizing the military is on a par with advocating pedophilia and gay marriage. The equation that Bush the Younger and his entourage are presenting is, if you criticize the president, you are criticizing the military, which means you are attacking the flag and thus thoroughly disloyal.

On the deck of the USS *Lincoln*, literally wrapped in the uniform, and metaphorically in the flag, the president as commander in chief once again reinforced the myth that the war in Iraq was part of the "war on terror," that started after September 11, by implying without actually stating, that Iraq was in some way culpable for the attacks on the World Trade Center. His target audience was not just the assembled ship's company but the proven high quotient of the gullible watching in the world outside.

He took the occasion to declare, "The liberation of Iraq is a crucial advance in the campaign against terror. We have removed an ally of al-Qaeda and cut off a source of terrorist funding. And this much is certain: No terrorist network will gain weapons of mass destruction from the Iraqi regime, because the regime is no more. In these nineteen months that changed the world, our actions have been focused and deliberate and proportionate to the offense. We have not forgotten the victims of September the 11, the last phone calls, the cold murder of children, the searches in the rubble. With those attacks, the terrorists and their supporters declared war on the United States, and war is what they got. Our war against terror is proceeding according to the principles that I have made clear to all. Any person involved in committing or planning terrorist attacks against the American people becomes an enemy of this country and a target of American justice."

As his own spokesmen have occasionally admitted, there never has been any serious evidence of any kind that Iraq was planning any type of attacks against the United States or its citizens, with the possible exception of an alleged plot against Bush Senior ten years ago, to which we shall return. As every serious student of the regime has continually pointed out, the secularist, nationalist, Ba'athist parties in Damascus and Baghdad, may indeed be fascist—but they are certainly not, in the term currently in vogue in U.S. intellectual circles, "Islamo"-Fascist.

However, as polls showed in September 2003, the White House's deft manipulation of their geopolitical ignorance, anti-Arab prejudice, and clever juxtaposition of pictures of Saddam Hussein with Osama bin Laden under the rubric of the "war on terror," had persuaded almost 70 percent of Americans. They believed that Baghdad was behind September 11 and that the war on Iraq was essentially payback

time. After all, their commander in chief—with his finger-
tips on the world's most comprehensive intelligence data
banks—was shocked when he discovered there were
Ba'athists in Damascus. Indeed, the Ba'athist Party had ruled
Syria for 40 years!

However, the commander in chief perpetrated an even
bigger lie than the causes of the war in Iraq. In fact, his
biggest fabulation was that the war was now over. To be fair,
it may not have been a lie as such—more a monumental
example of self-delusion and wish fulfillment. White House
officials briefed uncritical reporters that in his speech on the
Abraham Lincoln, that the president was making a statement
of the "commander's intent" to members of the air, land, and
naval forces in the Persian Gulf that the war was essentially
over, and that "this was an important moment of psychological closure."

"This is the military," a senior administration official,
who could not have had any military experience himself
unless it were Rumsfeld or Powell, condescendingly told
the *New York Times*,[3] "They don't just roll in one day.
Everything is defined. They need somebody to declare,
'This thing is over. . . .' This is the formalization that tells
everybody we're not engaged in combat anymore, we're
prepared for getting out."

As I write almost exactly a year later, with four times as
many American troops killed since it was "over," than while it
was being officially and formally waged, and with Halliburton
contracting for building massive bases all over Iraq, some of
the soldiery may have need of more than psychological closure

from the would-be warlord of the White House. By all accounts, many of the common soldiery even at that early stage were already thinking profoundly disloyal thoughts about the "formalization that tells everyone we're not engaged in combat," as they found bombs, mortars, and snipers somehow more convincing than White House platitudes.

3 TIMING

TIMING IS TO TELEVISION as location is to restaurants, but what's on the menu helps as well. The timing of Bush's speech for TV was wonderful. The trimmings attracted some considerable contumely within days, although of course the macrotiming, declaring the end of the war, was in retrospect also a tad premature.

To stage the spectacle in sweeps week when all the networks are doing their damnedest to get Americans in front of their screens, to time it for peak viewing on the major networks and provide wall-to-wall coverage for three hours of cable, on such a spectacular set, with so many extras provided gratis by the Pentagon; this was a coup de television of the first order!

The flight to the *Lincoln* was indeed a spectacular photo-op, carefully prepared and targeted, and in modern politics there are few leaders who, given the opportunity, would not try to boost their image with similar events, although few have the resources or the virtuoso technical skills and media savvy to produce such a technically perfect show.

Naturally, the usual partisan bickering ensued about the cost to the taxpayer but, after all, Bill Clinton had set the standard for abuse of presidential traveling with his innumerable fund-raising dinners and speeches to cities across the nation that so often happily coincided with official White House business. However, it was not the cost, but the whole conception that produced the most telling ripostes.

In fact, it was not really the expense that disturbed many of those who watched the pantomime with their jaws dropping. It was Bush the Younger's appropriation of others' sacrifice, the abuse of the memory of the hundreds of dead Americans and even of the thousands of Iraqis, for an early campaign commercial. Additionally, many found it unsettling that the president wrapped himself in the flag, and tried to associate himself with the military, not just as their titular commander in chief, but as a comrade in arms, a veteran who had suffered what they had suffered, who had shared the trenches and risked his life.

As Senator Robert C. Byrd of West Virginia, who so often has been almost the solo opposition in the Senate, declaimed, "As I watched the president's fighter jet swoop down onto the deck of the aircraft carrier *Abraham Lincoln*, I could not help but contrast the reported simple dignity of President Lincoln at Gettysburg with the flamboyant showmanship of President Bush aboard the USS *Abraham Lincoln*."

He added, "To me, it is an affront to the Americans killed

or injured in Iraq for the president to exploit the trappings of war for the momentary spectacle of a speech. I do not begrudge his salute to America's warriors aboard the carrier *Lincoln* . . . but I do question the motives of a deskbound president who assumes the garb of a warrior for the purposes of a speech."

As Byrd orated, when he saw the "Mission Accomplished" banner, "I could not help be reminded of the tobacco barns of my youth, which served as country road advertising backdrops for the slogans of chewing tobacco purveyors. I am loath to think of aircraft carrier being used as an advertising backdrop for a presidential political slogan, yet that is what I saw."

He concluded, "I believe that our military forces deserve to be treated with respect and dignity and not used as stage props to embellish a presidential speech." Oh, that it were just one presidential speech—but all over the U.S., even in Iraq, the uniforms have been the backdrop for such presidential speeches and photo opportunities.

And this is where Bush's chutzpah overshot the flight deck to fall into the sea of hypocrisy, because, of course, the landing on the aircraft carrier was the closest he had been to risking his life in uniform. And this "willingness to face danger," on his part was in no way "for his country and each other." It was for his own political advantage, which again was an uncanny parallel with his earlier faux military career.

When the government was drafting his contemporaries and sending them to Vietnam, he joined the Air National Guard in Texas, and ticked the box saying "no" to overseas service: a choice denied most of his contemporaries then, who did not have the Ivy League connections to enter such units.

More importantly, such choices are denied now to the National Guardsmen who were not only called up for service in Iraq, but have found their terms extended while they were out in the desert.

4 WRAPPING THE FLAG

PRESIDENT BUSH'S 2003 May Day flight was an outstanding, but by no means isolated, example of Bush's abuse by association of the military. As well as his "Loyalty Day" proclamation, he had tried for a double the day before his flight to California and the sunset glory of the USS *Abraham Lincoln*. He had attempted to conscript both God and the military on his side, by hosting 150 military chaplains for a prayer breakfast in the White House.

This Republican obsession with the military virtues is new, and contrived, and never more contrived than under Bush, who has tried to exorcise his somewhat ethereal military career by appearing whenever he can in front of made-to-order audiences at military bases or veterans' rallies. In eighteen months, more than one in three of his speeches and policy pronouncements were at military bases and veteran's gatherings.[4] Rallies, we would call them in another context and, once, ranks of uniforms drawn up to applaud a political leader would have sent shivers down the spine. Not for him; the unscripted happenstance of town hall meetings with voters or unchoreographed press conferences with inquisitive reporters: he is much happier surrounded by people in uniform, snappily saluting and calling him "Sir" and cheering dutifully whenever he pauses.

Typical was his staged ceremony at July 1, 2003, at the White House, where he welcomed thirty service people reenlisting. "Like many thousands of other soldiers, sailors, airmen, coastguardsmen, and marines who reenlist his year, these men and women are answering the highest call of citizenship. They have stood between the American people and the dangers of the world—and we are glad they are staying on duty," he declared, and went on say that "At present 230,000 Americans are serving inside or near Iraq. . . . As commander in chief I assure them, we will stay on the offensive against the enemy." There was no mention of the estimated 40,000 who, under "stop-loss orders," had been told they had stopped having or lost the option to leave at the end of their term of service!

Although, interestingly, he did not call himself "commander in chief" in his address to the nation on September 20, 2001, just after September 11, it is a phrase rarely off his lips when he speaks to the military, nor does he often miss an opportunity to don some form of military wear.

The pattern was set long ago. As far back as 1970, while campaigning for his father against Lloyd Bentsen, the future president wore his National Guard flight jacket, which is, of course, an uncanny precursor to that flight onto the deck of USS *Abraham Lincoln*.

Dressed in little brief authority, as a military person, he would then, as now, attract approbation in a way that a less sophisticated, less well-connected, long-haired draft evader would never do, which is why it is a wardrobe choice he now returns to often, from the decks of the USS *Abraham Lincoln* to the parade ground of forts and camps all over America.

Fort Hood, which, like so many U.S. military bases, is named after a Confederate general, John Bell Hood, is conveniently close to the "Western White House," Bush's dude ranch near Crawford, Texas. The massive bases, like Fort Hood, strewn across the South represent a major transfer of federal tax dollars from the former states of the Union to the old Confederacy, in a sense reparations for losing the Civil War. Naming them after Jefferson Davis's generals is the Old South's way of saying "thank you," to the Union government in between its extolling the virtues of low taxation and sturdy self-reliance.

Fort Hood is also the biggest base in the United States, home to over forty thousand troops. Bush went there January 3, 2003, even before the war, to gee up the soldiery in the huge camp, while appropriating the title he loves so much. "Wherever you may be sent, you can know that America is grateful, and your commander in chief is confident in your abilities and proud of your service," he told them, when only a few thousand had gone to the Iraqi region. None of this milquetoast civilian presidential stuff, you may notice.

The Department of Defense's Web site says the speech produced "more than twenty hooahs" for the president, who wore a fetching olive green windcheater emblazoned with the presidential seal and "Bush, U.S. Army" across his chest. In a way, he looked like Paddington Bear, who also had to be labeled in case he was lost, not least since the commander in chief blended so well with the ranks of military personnel dutifully lined up behind him.

Despite all those "hooahs," a more intrepid AP reporter actually noticed quite a lot of disquiet among the troops about the prospects of war, on both a personal level and on the larger political level. Modern soldiers are not totally isolated from the disquiet in the society that surrounds them.

The president is fond of this base, because it is so close to home. He was back in April, greeting returning prisoners of war and attending Easter services in the church there. (As governor he had already protested against the Wicca services held on the bases!) That meant he missed the Easter Egg Roll at the White House, but he was there in spirit. The feast on the lawn in Washington, commemorating the Prince of Peace, was angled at military children. Civilian children were left out, since the event was closed to the public.

"The youngsters in attendance were children of military families, including the sons and daughters of U.S. troops fighting in Iraq," said the GOP news service. Not only did the military offspring not get to see the president, since he was busy politicking at Fort Hood, the poor kids, some of them already separated from parents overseas, had to listen to Lynne Cheney, who read to them from her book *America: A Patriotic Primer,* which is surely a clear violation of the Constitution's prohibitions against cruel and unusual punishments, not to mention a form of abuse of juveniles. (One cannot help but wonder at the title for a vice president's wife. Is it the vice-lady?)

At the Fort Hood Easter services, the commander in chief met with two recently returned POWs from Iraq, and threw an arm around the shoulder of one of them, Senior Warrant Officer David S. Williams. As Bush told reporters, "He is going to go see his children for the first time since he was captured. He hasn't even seen his children. So if you ask him questions, don't make it long, because, see, we're holding a dad up from hugging two children." Of course, being held to be a prop for the photo-op for the President had not kept the warrant officer from his children at all. Any more than waiting offshore for the presidential jet landing was going to keep the crew of the USS *Lincoln* from theirs on May 1.

There were not as many waiting to greet him at Easter as on his New Year's visit: By then, half the forty thousand troops normally housed at the base were in Iraq missing their Easter eggs. When the *Washington Post* checked into the neighborhood early in 2004, thirty-five of them were never coming back—all but one of them killed after the president had made his "formalization that tells everybody we're not engaged in combat anymore," the previous May.[5]

Unctuously, in the face of such casualties, the first lady returned to the base March 8, 2004, and told a group of military wives that she knows what it's like "having your life turned upside down because the man you love wants to serve the country he loves." At least she did not wear a uniform for the occasion—and did not mention Vietnam and the various forms of "service."

The Armed Forces Press Service reported the first lady telling the group that she and the president have visited with soldiers at bases all over the world, but that fewer visits have inspired them more than those to Walter Reed Army Medical Center in Washington, D.C. "These brave men and women were lying in hospital beds wounded and broken, yet they talked with enthusiasm about returning to their units," she said. Good Soldier Schweik would be weeping tears of laughter.

A random trawl of the newswires and Defense Department White House archives produces the same dazzling camouflage. On August 14, 2003, the president himself was telling it to the marines, at Miramar Marine base in California, "I am proud to be the commander in chief of such a fabulous group of men and women who wear our uniform." At Fort Polk Louisiana, he met with "military personnel" on February 17, 2004, and said, "What a week. First NASCAR (*Applause*.) — and today, Fort Polk, Louisiana (*Applause*.)."

In a way, he was also appealing to another audience since Fort Polk was named after the Right Reverend Leonidas Polk, the first Episcopal bishop of the Diocese of Louisiana—and, of course, a Confederate general. To add to the cleverly concocted web of duckspeak, as at most of these speeches, he repeatedly invoked the soldiers' role in the "war on terrorism."

His speech on the first anniversary of the beginning of the war in Iraq was also before a "conscripted" audience at Fort

Campbell in Kentucky. There, twenty thousand men and women of the 101st Airborne paraded with little handheld flags in their hands and jumbo-sized banners flying overhead, to provide a backdrop to the president's latest photo-op. Fort Campbell, unusually, takes its name from a Unionist general but, since he won his spurs beating up on Mexicans, I suppose the South let the Pentagon get away with it—just this once.

For the occasion, the president himself, once again, wore a signature military jacket with "George W. Bush, commander in chief" over his heart. He forgot the previous year's "formalized ending" of the war on the USS *Lincoln* as he used the occasion to thank those in Congress who supported his $87 billion emergency spending measure for Iraq, better characterized as the Halliburton Booster Bill, Bush presented it as "meeting the needs of our troops in the field right now." And, coincidentally, as the networks and cable channels showed the president basking in the approval and comradeship of the uniformed masses, his reelection campaign released its Kerry-knocking campaign, accusing his Democratic challenger of voting against the measure, and therefore voting against defense and security. No matter that the same week the Pentagon withheld payments from Halliburton for overcharging on the bid-free contract they had secured to "meet the needs of our troops."

Maladroitly, Kerry himself was shown skiing at his home, rather than wearing a uniform he was somewhat more entitled to wear than was his tormentor. Unable to defend himself on the economy, on health care, the deficit, or job-creation, on most of which the Democrats have better poll ratings, Bush was playing to what he and his strategists perceive as the Republican strength, their identification with the military, with security, and, thus, defense against the latest boogey— terrorism.

Even if his visit to the Normandy beaches for the sixtieth anniversary of the D-day landings in June does represent an advance on the Neanderthal wing of his party that seriously proposed digging up the bodies of American war dead and bringing them home from France, one felt forebodingly sure that the occasion would show the commander in chief again parading his martial virtues in front of the world in general— and Midwestern and Southern white conservative voters in particular.

We should not think that it is just serving soldiers he likes to command. There are twenty-five million veterans out there, so he is as eager to associate with them as with present soldiers. For example, on Veterans Day 2003 he began at 11:38 AM at Arlington National Cemetery where he announced that "our veterans include more than eleven million men and women from the conflicts of Korea and Vietnam," and "more than twenty-five million Americans wear the proud title of veteran or retired military." What does that mean . . . is there a subtle blurring of the distinction between those who fought and those who *served* as Bush claims to have done?

In a pathetic attempt to identify with his audience, Bush continued: "Every veteran has lived by a strict code of disciple. Every veteran understands the meaning of personal accounta- bility and loyalty, and shared sacrifice. From the moment you repeated the oath, to the day of your honorable discharge, your

time belonged to America. Your country came before all else."
It is interesting of course, the expedient way in which the cult
of the veteran, irreproachable and perfect, protects himself
from criticism. As we shall see, until the time he contrived an
honorable discharge, Bush's time belonged to a succession of
Republican election candidates, and to himself.

He then went on to the Heritage Foundation, the right-
wing think tank, telling them, "The title of veteran is a term
of great respect in American, all who *served*, whether for a
few years or for many, have put the nation's needs above their
own." (There's that *served* word again . . .)

The speeches of this period are also interesting for how
they keep a lie in orbit. Even though the White House had
officially dropped blaming Iraq for September 11, he could
put the same canard in the mouth of anonymous veterans,
confident that it would thus be irrefutable. At the cemetery,
he quoted, "One young man serving in Iraq recently said this:
'We in the military signed up and pledged to protect this
great country of ours from enemies foreign and domestic.
We're fighting so that the next generation might never have
to experience anything like September 11, 2001.'" Of course,
that quote was greeted with uncritical applause.

A few days later, he was at it again, issuing a proclamation
of National Employer Support of the Guard and Reserve
Week, "in honor of employers across America who have
shown their support for our National Guardsmen and
reservists. . . . Employers have shown great consideration for
their workers who have been called to duty and great support
for the nation's defense. These companies have the gratitude

of our nation, they have the gratitude of the commander in chief." Oh how he *loves* that title . . .

However, while those that do the right thing may get presidential gratitude, they are unlikely to face federal wrath. About thirteen hundred National Guardsmen and reservists filed complaints with the Department of Labor in the fiscal year that ended September 2003, alleging discrimination at work when they returned to their regular jobs after their tours of duty. That was up by four hundred complaints from 2001—and that is before the bulk of the guardsmen have actually made it back to be discriminated against!

Elaine Chao, the Labor Secretary, launched a televised public-service announcement, reminding employers of their obligations to rehire returning soldiers, but it does not threaten penalties, which may be just as well, since we have yet to hear of any actual prosecutions from the notoriously docile department.

5 POTEMKIN VILLAGE

IT IS ALMOST STANDARD operating procedure in military bases for the officers and personnel to put on a good show for visiting dignitaries, let alone one who calls himself the commander in chief. But there were several occasions, notably his flying visit to Iraq for Thanksgiving 2003 as well as the swoop down on the deck of the USS *Lincoln* that stand out in their manipulation of imagery, scenery, and context.

In the old Russian Empire, Count Gregory Potemkin used to pretty up villages that his lover Czarina Catherine was going to travel through. The idea was to impress her with the happiness and prosperity of the peasantry—regardless of the reality of the condition, thus giving rise to the phrase "Potemkin village."

We should perhaps be glad that in these more democratic days, our rulers have reversed the direction. The literally flying visit to Iraq for Thanksgiving 2003 and the landing on the USS *Abraham Lincoln* were parts of an elaborate illusion that the president and his cabal have conjured up to persuade the peasantry, the voters, that their leader has martial virtues and experience—regardless of the reality.

At least he did not claim to fly Air Force One to Iraq, as he implied he had the flight to USS *Abraham Lincoln*. The "yes, I flew it" comment to Fox TV was interesting, since his license to fly jets had expired over thirty years before when he, unexplainedly rather than inexplicably, had failed to turn up for his medical in the Air National Guard back in 1972. In fact, by many accounts, he had failed to turn up for the National Guard at all for most of that year.

To stage the landing on the *Lincoln*, a team under Special Assistant to the President and Deputy Director of Communication for Production Scott Sforza, had been embedded on the carrier for several days, preparing for the event with consummate stagecraft. He even made sure that the crew members who backdropped the president had coordinated their shirt colors for the show. The White House's Chief of Staff Andy Card, Spokesman Ari Fleischer, and National Security Adviser Condoleezza Rice were with the crew on the flight deck, brought in on planes ahead of the performance.

Originally, the White House claimed that the reason for the president to land by jet on the deck was because the *Abraham Lincoln* was out of helicopter range and did not want to inconvenience the returning crew. Then they had to admit soon afterwards that it *was* in helicopter range, thereby implicitly admitting that the whole spectacle was mounted for the president's political advantage.

Indeed, the carrier was only thirty miles from land, and had actually veered away so that it was not in sight. An equally backtracking White House Press Secretary Ari Fleischer claimed that "The ship did make much faster progress than anticipated," but then veered and alleged that the ship had come inshore because of bad weather, so the White House had stuck with the original plan for a jet landing.

The president, he said, "wanted to see it as realistically as possible. And that's why, once the initial decision was made to fly out on the Viking, even when a helicopter option became doable, the president decided instead he wanted to still take the Viking."[6] He wanted to land on the *Lincoln* "in a manner that would allow him to see an arrival on a carrier the same way pilots got to see an arrival on a carrier."

In fact, from all this obfuscation, it seems clear that in contrast with the president's stated concern about inconveniencing crew, they and their ship were deliberately held offshore simply to provide the carefully contrived photo opportunity for the president.

As we shall see repeatedly, in reality, the president has a somewhat patrician disdain for the welfare, rights, and opinions of those who actually do the fighting. Whether extending terms, skimping on their equipment, skimping on reinforcements, risking their lives unnecessarily, or cutting their benefits when they retire, Lieutenant Bush U.S.A.F. Reserve Rtd., has let down those whose support and validation he craves. His support for "the military" has manifested itself in shoveling taxpayers' and bond-buyers' cash into the maws of what his distinguished Republican predecessor General Dwight D. Eisenhower called "the Military-Industrial Complex"—the Halliburtons, Boeings, and Bechtels.

Then the president went for the famous Thanksgiving turkey in Iraq on November 27, 2003—even further to fly for a photo-op than the USS *Abraham Lincoln*, but almost as contrived. Twenty-seven hours of flying for two-and-a-half hours of strutting *with* a turkey instead of *like* one—and, of course, he wore a fetching army exercise jacket with a First Armored Division patch.

It was an even more elaborate a photo-op than the *Lincoln*, and the White House did its damnedest to show how brave and intrepid the president was sharing the perils of the soldiery— even if it did rather contradict the other message they had been pushing: that Iraq had been pacified and was now entirely safe. However, in the brave new world of American politics, doublethink, believing two contradictory things at the same time, is an elementary feat.

When he reached Iraq, the doublespeak outquacked the duckspeak. Referring to the former regime, he claimed that his administration "looked at the intelligence information and we saw danger. Members of Congress looked at the same intelligence, and they saw danger. The United Nations Security Council looked at the intelligence, and saw danger."

One would never guess that the Security Council had refused to authorize the invasion, or that just before he went to Iraq, U.S. weapons inspector, David Kay, had gone to

Congress and admitted he had not found any tangible evidence to back up all this "intelligence."

To compound it, Bush said that the UN Security Council had demanded a full accounting of Saddam Hussein's weapons programs or he would face serious consequences, which is true. However, then he claimed that "Saddam Hussein chose defiance," which is not what Hans Blix, the head of the UN weapons inspectors, was saying, and nor was anyone else but the U.S. and its closest friends on the Security Council. It may have taken the threat of invasion, but Saddam was actually cooperating with the weapons inspectors—to the frustration of the Pentagon, the White House, and Number 10 Downing Street.

To build up the cloak-and-dagger image of the intrepid commander in chief risking his life to be with the troops, Dan Bartlett at the White House circulated the tale that Air Force One was spotted by a British Airways pilot who radioed the cockpit, "Did I just see Air Force One?" The tale was that they almost cancelled the mission was until the quick-thinking pilot of Air Force One passed himself off as "Gulfstream 5." Maybe the White House was worried that airliners from Air France, Lufthansa, or some other "Old" European airline may have intercepted and rammed a plane carrying the world's least popular potentate?

The story splashed across Middle America, and in the souvenir shops in Bush's hometown Crawford, Texas, they guffawed Texan style and tried to make a quick buck out of the tall tale. As Reuters breathlessly reported, "The midair encounter, which aides say nearly prompted the president to call off the trip, became an instant news sensation, memorialized by tourist pins which went on sale at a store in Crawford within hours of Bush's return to his Texas ranch."

Sadly, British Airways is less malleable than the British Prime Minister. Just as the White House press officers were doubtless high-fiving each other in joy at how many hits their story had got, the grinches at BA denied that any of their pilots had had any such conversation. So the White House corrected itself, and said that the conversation was not between a BA speedbird and Air Force One, but that the presidential carrier's cockpit eavesdropped on an exchange between the BA flight and the British control tower. Still mean, nasty, and superciliously British, BA said they had had no planes in the vicinity at the time.

So that story also plummeted like a lead balloon orbiting a black hole. The White House shoved it down the memory hole and tried again. The conversation had taken place between British air traffic control and another plane while Air Force One was "off the western coast of England." In fact, they should have consulted First Lt. Bush, who got much better grades for navigation on his National Guard aptitude test than he did for piloting. Air Force One was actually over the North Sea on the *eastern* coast of England. And by then the White House was suggesting it may have been a German charter jet, not a British Airways plane that did the spotting.

In fact, if it existed, and if it did spot Air Force One, then it may well have been in danger because of the subterfuge. David Luxton, head of the British air traffic controllers' union, was angry because the White House had claimed the

flight was a tiny Gulfstream executive rather than a massive
Boeing 747, since the deceit breached International Civil Aviation Organization regulations, and posed a safety hazard. "If
the president's men who did this can dupe air traffic control,
what's to stop a highly organized terrorist group from duping
air traffic control?"Luxton asked.

He explained that the Gulfstream is much more maneu-
verable than a 747, which means controllers could have
assumed the president's plane could take evasive action in
event of an impending collision, while the vortex left in the
wake of a jumbo could jeopardize smaller planes if the misled
controllers had told them to follow it.

The colorizing of Bush's otherwise colorless life did not
stop in the dark night six miles over the cold North Sea. After
Bush had arrived in Iraq, for the "surprise" visit, the photo-
opportunity of him holding up the turkey went 'round the
world. Only later did it become apparent that this iconic,
albeit nonstrutting, bird, surrounded by all the customary
trimmings, was in fact an artificial showpiece, provided by
Halliburton for display, and presumably for just this occasion.

Faced with this evidence of Potemkinization, the White
House spin doctors then claimed that the plastic poultry just
happened to be there, and the president, who just happened to
be wearing a military jacket, just happened to pick the tray
with the turkey just as a photographer just happened to be
passing. It was just too much happenstance for a carefully
scripted and choreographed presidential visit.

In fact, the armed forces newspaper *Stars and Stripes*
proved less gullible than the wire services and the average

small-town newspaper and blew the whistle. It reported that predictably, the cheering soldiers who greeted him on his "surprise" visit to Baghdad had been carefully chosen, while others who showed up for their own turkey dinner were turned away.

Army First Armored Division officials told that the *Stars and Stripes* that, "for security reasons, only those preselected got into the facility during Bush's visit. . . . The soldiers who dined while the president visited were selected by their chain of command, and were notified a short time before the visit."

As with the sailors, who, ending their ten-month tour on the USS *Abraham Lincoln*, were kept dallying offshore on May Day to provide a presidential backdrop, soldiers in Iraq went hungry on Thanksgiving, so the commander in chief could get his picture taken. Sgt. Loren Russell wrote to the *Stars and Stripes* describing the heroism of his men and women and added, "Imagine their dismay when they walked fifteen minutes to the Bob Hope Dining Facility, only to find that they were turned away from their evening meal because they were in the wrong unit. . . . They understand that President Bush ate there and that upgraded security was required. But why were only certain units turned away?"

His men instead decided to grouse with each other, and "eat MREs, even after the chow hall was reopened for 'usual business' at 9 PM As a leader myself, I'd guess that other measures could have been taken to allow for proper security and still let the soldiers have their meal."

We can be cynical. Indeed far too many of us are, and assume that politicians lie. But even in America, not many of them are quite so blatant about it. As McClellan explained the changes in the White House story about the alleged BA Air Force One spotting, he obfuscated "I don't think everybody was clear on exactly how that conversation happened." But then he confessed that the White House was merely trying to be helpful to journalists, saying "What we always try to do . . . is to provide you a little color of important events."

There is a good reason why Bush the Younger reincarnates these creative combinations of Baron von Munchausen and Walter Mitty in his press office. His own actual life has not lived up to the image that he would like, and which he and his team think the voters would like.

6 SOLDIER OF FORTUNE

SINCE HE HAS PERSUADED the vast majority of Americans, if not the citizens of any other country in the world, that Saddam Hussein was responsible for the attacks on the World Trade Center, perhaps we should not be surprised at George W. Bush's success in passing himself off as a veteran with so many Americans, including many who are actually combat-seasoned veterans themselves.

Senator Bob Kerrey (D-Nebraska), bearer of the Medal of Honor, represents what we may have to assume is more than an enlightened minority of vets. "It upsets me, when someone says, 'Vote for me, I was in the military,' when in fact he got into the military in order to avoid serving in the military, to avoid service that might have taken him into the war. And then he didn't even show up for duty."

In the official bio at the State Department it was recorded that that "George W. Bush was commissioned as second lieutenant and spent two years on active duty, flying F-102 fighter interceptors. For almost four years after that, he was on a part-time status, flying occasional missions to help the Air National Guard keep two of its F-102s on round-the-clock service." As we shall soon see this is a considerable exaggeration of the truth.

After the *Boston Globe* raised the issue, the bio was amended and currently reads that the president "received a bachelor's degree from Yale University in 1968, then served as an F-102 fighter pilot in the Texas Air National Guard," a contraction which, while it retracted the lie direct is still a lie circumstantial, an implied continuing attempt to appropriate a military mystique for the president. As a British politician once said, this description "contains a misleading impression, not a lie. It is being economical with the truth."[7]

In many ways, the disturbing issue is not the nugatory unreality of his service: it is the cultivation of this false self-image and his projection of himself like some Latin-American caudillo. Neither the dissimulation, nor the confabulated image that he has tried to conjure up with it, represents what most of the world wants from the man heading the world's only superpower.

So where does it all come from? In fact, there appears to be a complex set of reasons, ranging from the sociological to the psychopathological on to the pragmatically and cynically political.

As so often, mistaking the form for the reality, it would appear that George W. Bush had wanted to follow in the contrail of his father, who had also been a pilot. The difference is that Bush the Elder had enlisted as soon he reached the age of eighteen, and went into the navy, where he risked his life in combat. Bush the Elder did pull strings to jump the queue, but as nepotism goes that is surely less culpable than his son's.

Some Bush-the-Younger apologists have pointed out that flying fighter planes is a dangerous job, which is probably true, but even they have to admit, that it is a lot more dangerous when people are shooting at you, and Lieutenant Bush Jr. had made sure that that was an extremely unlikely contingency.

The other difference is that timing thing. Bush Senior enlisted at the first opportunity he had, at the age of eighteen, going straight from his Andover prep school to be the youngest pilot in the navy. He flew in the Pacific and was shot down. One can churlishly suspect that he was trying to put big distance between himself and his father, Prescott Bush, whose Union Bank Corporation was taken over by the Custodian of Enemy Property for its Nazi connections. In a foretaste of the Bush dynasty's control of the memory holes, this embarrassing tie was not mentioned when Prescott Bush was running for the Senate—and certainly not widely circulated afterwards.

In contrast to his father's unseemly haste for combat, Bush the Younger took his time. At Andover, his undistinguished career—arranging stickball leagues and acting as cheerleader for the team—brought him notice without any significant intellectual achievement. At Yale, four years of rugby, more traditional American football, and partying culminated in being tapped for the Skull and Bones secret society, which he was to say later was "so secret, I can't say anything more."

Doctor Samuel Johnson hazarded that the prospect of

being hanged would "concentrate a man's mind wonderfully." So as the year of his graduation began, Bush the
Younger's mind, never totally on his studies, began to focus
on military service.

There were an amazing number of ways out for anyone
with money and the know-how, ranging from Arlo Guthrie's
littering conviction to medical deferment, the road taken by
24.2 percent of those examined in 1966 but rising to 40.7 percent in July 1969 as its potential became obvious. Of course,
there was always the option of outright illegality. You could
buy papers to get an exemption, from, for example, the New
York draft board official convicted of selling deferments and
exemptions for anything up to $30,000 each.

Then there was student deferment. One can only imagine
that one point on which Bush the Younger had in agreement
with the student protestors against the Vietnam War was
cursing out Lyndon Baines Johnson. In an egalitarian move,
genuinely concerned at the class selectivity of the draft, LBJ had
stopped the graduate-student deferment, which was boiling
down the draft so that it increasingly applied only to those who
could not afford to go to college or pay for a specialist.

If graduate deferment had remained in place, presumably
George W. Bush would have rushed to serve his country at
Harvard Business School immediately. With his football,
rugby, and similar sporting record, it would have been somewhat surprising for George W. Bush to take the medical disability road—but by no means unprecedented.

However, even at this early stage, Bush Jr. showed some
of the can-do firmness he likes to project now. Men who

signed up for the National Guard were not drafted. Such was the martial fervor in the state where they remember the Alamo so fondly that there was an eighteen-month waiting list to join the Texas National Guard. Another hundred thousand would-be summer soldiers and sunshine patriots queued up nationally to join the state militias mentioned in the constitution.

As they waited patiently yet apprehensively in line for their tickets, the sharp visioned would have seen a supersonic Bush the Younger shooting over their heads: his application to join the Air National Guard was accepted the same day he made it.

Like the Battle of Waterloo, it was a damn near-run thing. He only had twelve days before his student deferment expired. But, even so, it was too quick for the unit commander, who mounted an action replay of George W. Bush taking his oath the following day to allow a photo-op of the young scion of the Texas aristocracy joining his already elite-filled unit. As we have seen, it was to be only the first of many contrived military portraits for the young aspirant pilot.

Bush got the last of the four pilots' slots available. There had clearly been some thought on this matter, implying that the last-minute rush was premeditated, at least in the sense that the Bushes knew it was a done deal. After all, the first moves had been made back in December, when various versions indicated that over Christmas an anxious young George was canvassing the Texas cocktail-party circuit.

In his autohagiography, *A Charge to Keep*, he says, "I knew I would serve. Leaving the country to avoid the draft was not an option for me; I was too conservative and too traditional.

My inclination was to support the government and the war until proven wrong, and that only came later, as I realized we could not explain the mission, had no exit strategy, and did not seem to be fighting to win."[8]

With similar economy for the truth he says that when he was home in Houston for Christmas, "I heard from contemporaries that there were openings in the Texas Air National Guard, and I called to ask about them. There were several openings, I was told, because many people who wanted to go into the guard were unwilling to spend the almost two years of full-time duty needed for pilot training."[9] Ah, such economy with the truth!

In fact, Senator Bob Kerrey of Nebraska alleges that there were five hundred applicants waiting to get into the Air National Guard in Texas. Also, the "someone," either Bush or his father called to ask was Colonel Walter "Buck" Staudt who was the commander of 111th Tactical Recon Texas Air National Guard. Texas circles knew this unit specifically as "Air Canada," since joining it had all the advantages of fleeing north of the border as far as service in Vietnam was concerned, and none of the political or meteorological downside and was generically considered a "champagne unit" since its personnel was so rich and well-connected.

In the unlikely event of the ghosts of Santana and Zapata ever rising on the Texas border to reclaim the Lone Star State for the United States of Mexico, then the Texas National Guard may have seen some tough fighting. But there was no way they were ever going to Vietnam, hence its popularity.

The unit in which Bush the Younger had "heard there

were some vacancies" was a sort of reservation for the endangered aristocracy of Texas. The Bushes were not alone in competing for the "Duke of Plaza-Toro" prize for rear-echelon bravery. Seven Dallas Cowboys, and the sons of Senator Lloyd Bentsen (D-Texas) and Governor John Connally shared the mess with the offspring of Bush family chum and Texan oilman Sid Adger, who seems to have been the one who made the moves for Bush.

Adger called Speaker of the Texas House Ben Barnes who in turn pulled the strings on General James Rose, the officer commanding the Texas Air National Guard in its relentless struggle to keep Texas safe from sneak Mexican attacks. Usefully, Barnes's aide, Nick Kralj, also doubled up as the aide to General Rose. In best *Dynasty*-like fashion, there was a leadership struggle going on for command of the Texas Air National Guard with Rose's position under threat. It would have been a foolhardy incumbent who did not take the hint. There is little about Texas politics to suggest that subtlety of hints was common stock in trade.

Demonstrating the cozy nature of politics in those days, Barnes was the Democratic Speaker, so this was totally bipartisan operation. This is of course what protected Bush the Younger in later elections. There was nothing he could have been accused of that would not have caused serious blowback in the faces of his opponents.

The chronic amnesia that afflicts Bush has worked its erasing magic again about this. When the *Dallas Morning News* asked then-governor of Texas George W. Bush, about approaches by the alleged fixers, Barnes and Adger,[10] he denied it. "I have no idea and I don't believe so. I applied to be a pilot in the guard and I met the requirements and the people who decided I was going to be in the guard have said publicly that there was no influence. All I know is anybody named George Bush did not ask him for help," the governor and GOP presidential front-runner pronounced in unmistakable Bush family syntax while campaigning in New Hampshire.

But amusingly enough, despite the chumminess in Texas politics, there is occasionally a fallout over the spoils, and litigation dragged Speaker Barnes to the edge of perjury. In 1999, the former Texas Lottery director, Laurence Littwin, had sued the State over his dismissal which he said was because he had given the contract to run it to a politically disfavored company. He had called Barnes as witness to back his story that he was the victim of a deal to keep a company—GTech—running the lottery in return for Barnes's silence about how he helped Bush get into the guard. Bush was now the governor of Texas.

Barnes had been lobbyist for the company, but he and the Bushes point out that he had stopped working for them before Littwin was either hired or fired. However, the cynical may think that his $23 million payoff from GTech, who run lotteries in over three dozen states, could indeed have created some residual bonds of sympathy.

In the end, under oath, and mindful of the penalties for perjury, Barnes had to admit that he had indeed called to ease the way for Bush into the guard, but said it was in response to a request from Sid Adger, who was now fortuitously dead and so unable to challenge the Bush family's denial that they had made any calls.

Barnes's statement, taken as vindication by the Bush family and campaign, and for which he was thanked for his candor by George W., was explicit that he had not been approached by any member of the Bush family for special treatment, but by Sid Adger.

Bush the Younger wrote gratefully, "Dear Ben: Don Evans reported your conversation. Thank you for your candor and for killing the rumor about you and dad ever discussing my status. Like you, he never remembered any conversation. I appreciate your help." (It is as well that Americans do not speak the president's English the way that Brits are supposed to speak the queen's English!)

Who knows? When King Henry asked in a loud voice whether anyone would rid him of this troublesome priest, he later feigned amazement that two ambitious knights who had overheard him rode out to slaughter St. Thomas a Beckett. Maybe at some cocktail party one of the Bush clan just looked up at the ceiling and wished that someone could get young George (or horror, maybe even little Googen, his baby name!) into the National Guard.

However, Barnes' belated confession forced Bush spokespeople to retract their original denial that the governor had had special treatment. Conveniently, the person Barnes admitted tapping for the favor, Brig. Gen. James Rose is also dead, and as unable to comment as Adger.

In some ways it is nice to note that memory problems, like wobbly syntax, run in the family. When pressed, Jean Becker,

Bush senior's spokeswoman at the time, said he was "almost positive" that he and Mr. Adger never discussed the guard matter. "He is fairly certain—I mean he doesn't remember everything that happened in the 1960s . . ." she said. In any case, Bush Sr. and Adger were very close. Indeed, Ms. Becker acknowledged that "President Bush [the Elder] knew Sid Adger well. He loved him." Adger may have needed only that hint.

Indeed Bush Jr. himself conceded that he knew Adger socially at the time, and admitted that he met Col. "Buck" Staudt, the commander of the VIP unit in late 1967, during Christmas vacation of his senior year, called him later, and—in Bush's words—"found out what it took to apply." Staudt claims that he, not General Rose (who he later replaced), was the one who made the decision on admissions anyway.

Bush's ghostwriter and then-spokeswoman Karen Hughes filled in some of the memory gaps. He "heard from friends while he was home over the Christmas break that . . . Colonel Staudt was the person to contact." She says that Bush doesn't recall, as in fact his memory often does not serve him well just who his "friends" were. However, it is a matter of record that Sid Adger was also a friend of Staudt, and had recently held a luncheon honoring Staudt and his unit for winning an air force commendation. Indeed Adger's own sons had already traipsed up the silver spoon road and had joined the 111th.

Close up, the picture may be confusing, but from a little distance, it is clear that young Bush was happily bound up in a web of nepotism and mutual back-scratching, or Texas politics as it was then.

Having plotted the course, young George took the aptitude test for air force officers on January 19, 1968, in New Haven. Who knows, maybe at that time, he did really want to follow his father's contrails, and be a hotshot pilot and war hero. Or maybe he had learnt that graduate student deferment from the draft was going to finish on February 17, and so his mind was concentrated on the issue—apropos Dr. Johnson—"wonderfully."

The test showed him with a grade of 25 percent for pilot aptitude, 50 for navigation, and 95 for officer quality. One suspects that you get 75 percent for simply answering yes to questions like, "Is your family rich, politically connected, and did you go to Yale or Harvard?" Apparently the average is 88 percent, which says a lot about the stringency of the filters for officer material. Indeed, the tests could not be too hard because he scored an impressive 85 percent on verbal aptitude, which leads one to suspect that it must have been a multiple-choice test, since one cannot really see him getting that score if he had had to write a sentence.

Those low scores may have caused some anxious moments since outside the ivory towers of Yale and the concrete blocks of Austin, Texas, history was moving in its habitually discommoding way. Less than two weeks after he took the test, Vietnam changed—forever. On the night of January 30, General Giap launched the Tet Offensive, which stormed into South Vietnamese cities, even taking the American embassy in Saigon.

In fact, some Vietnamese sources suggest that it was a foul-up worthy of the Pentagon. North Vietnam had recently changed the lunar calendar it used to calculate Tet, but had not checked with its Vietcong units in the south, so the offensive lost its holiday surprise as different military regions attacked on different days.

In retrospect, the Tet Offensive was a military defeat for the Vietcong and North Vietnamese Army, but that was not the way it looked at the time. Regardless, it was a political victory for Giap and Hanoi, the beginning of the end for the U.S. in Vietnam. With a panglossian optimism presaging current official pronouncements in Iraq, the U.S. had been assuring everyone that the war was under control, so it was a great shock for American civilians, not least perhaps those who, like George Bush, were imminently *ex*-civilians and did not usually question their government's rosy optimism on such issues. The battle raged for weeks, with literally suicidal courage on the part of the Vietcong, resulting in heavy casualties on both sides.

The aspirant airman went for a medical examination at the air force base in Massachusetts on February 21 of that year, and was deemed "not qualified" because of problems with his teeth. So Bush visited a dentist in New Haven on March 7. The dentist pulled one tooth from the future president and put a filling in another. In view of his later flaunting of his Air National Guard experience as military "service," perhaps it is worthwhile recording that real air force personnel refer to them, and not affectionately, as FANGERS—"fucking Air National Guarders."

A month later Bush's medical file was updated to show him

as "medically qualified." As he sharpened his fangs, the Tet Offensive was winding down. While he nursed his toothache, U.S. and South Vietnamese government forces had retaken Hue and the U.S. command there had requested 206,000 more troops (presumably including air force personnel).

Could it be that the sight of such mayhem on television caused the young George W. Bush to temper his ambitions of emulating his father? By the time he ticked the box for not volunteering, he had obviously made a decision, but when or why is of course a mystery.

Just weeks before he went to the National Guard recruitment depot in Houston, the Pentagon had called up 24,500 men from the reserves. As we noted, with only twelve days to go before he was due down at the draft office to do his legal duty, he put in his application to Staudt, where it seems he was confident of acceptance.

Adger's son Steve, also a noncombat veteran of the 147th, told the *Dallas Morning News*, "He may have done it or he may not have done it, but it didn't take Gen. Staudt. I mean here George W. shows up, a graduate of Yale, a great guy, son of a congressman, that's all he needed."

Indeed, not only did he have a red carpet laid down to the door, but Bush the Younger was on a fast track as soon as he was inside it. His buddy, sorry, commander, approved him for a "direct appointment," which got him a commission without having to go through the usual (and difficult) Officer Candidate School.

This procedure was generally reserved for applicants with exceptional experience or skills, such as ROTC training or engineering, medical or aviation skills. Bush had none and an incredibly low pilot aptitude score. But just as in the old days in England where attendance at Eton automatically made you officer material, Bush's silver spoon transmuted into officers pips.

His blue blood from the East, and the red blood of the Bush family co-option by the Texas oil dynasties, obviously offered advantages and qualities that outweighed minor flaws, like only scoring 25 percent on the pilot aptitude test. It is lucky that he was not flying too far from his home state of Texas as well, with that not too impressive grade on his navigation test. As President George W. Bush and his party decry the inequity of affirmative action for minorities, we should pause and reflect on how many bonus points his bluish blood added to his grades to get him through.

It is not as if the 75 percent or just above that he scraped at Yale was in anyway significant as an academic record. Observers of Yale suggest that for "issue due a legacy," students with wealthy fathers who went before them, 75 was the minimum grade that all those endowment dollars bought. In between the various forms of football, touch, rugby, contact, and so on that the ex-cheerleader indulged in, his transcript proudly recorded his work on the Armour Council at Yale. This was not some form of ROTC, with jousts on the lawn. My Yale sources tell me they were the guys who made sure enough kegs were rolled in for the parties.

As Bush the Younger raced through the ranks he signed a "Statement of Intent" to reassure anxious taxpayers that the hundreds of thousands of dollars that they were spending on this pilot would not go to waste. He declared that when he had finished pilot training, "I plan to return to my unit and fulfill my obligation to the utmost of my ability. I have applied for plot training with the goal of making flying a lifetime pursuit." Ah, but where would he fly?

"I spent 55 weeks on active duty learning to fly and graduated in December 1969," he later wrote. But by the end of the year, after his training, as some of the toughest fighting of Vietnam War raged in places like Saigon, young Bush took two months leave of absence to go work on the Florida senatorial campaign of Edward Gurney. By then there were 526,000 U.S. troops in Vietnam.

7 QUANTUM VIETNAM

GEORGE W. BUSH WAS not one of those half million plus servicemen in Vietnam. Nor was he likely to be, as he near enough admitted with unprecedented candor in times past, before, perhaps, the GOP abuse of Clinton sensitized him to the political dangers of draft dodging. In 1989, he told the *Lubbock Avalanche-Journal*, "I'm saying to myself, 'What do I want to do?' I think I don't want to be an infantry guy as private in Vietnam. What I do decide to want to do is learn to fly."

In 1994, he told the *Houston Chronicle*, "I was not prepared to shoot my eardrum out with a shotgun in order to get a deferment. Nor was I willing to go to Canada. So I chose to better myself by learning how to fly airplanes."

"I don't want to play like I was somebody out there marching when I wasn't. It was either Canada or the service. . . . Somebody said the guard was looking for pilots. All I know is, there weren't that many people trying to be pilots,"[11] he told the *Fort Worth Star Telegram* in 1989.

Setting aside the thought that five hundred anxious young potential draftees in line for a couple of pilots' slots is a tad more than "not that many," implicit in these statements was a determination not to go to Vietnam and risk his life in dubious battle. That was even though he was busily working to elect candidates who were sending his less-connected contemporaries to do just that. Also, he did tick the box that said "do not volunteer" for overseas military service, so he certainly did not want to be a pilot in Vietnam anyway. That tick caused and still causes him some serious problems.

As Colin Powell said in his memoirs (before joining Bush's cabinet), "I can never forgive a leadership that said, in effect: These young men—poor, less-educated, less-privileged—are expendable (someone described them as 'economic cannon fodder'), but the rest are too good to risk."

Powell added, presciently and inconveniently, "I am angry that so many of the sons of the powerful and well-placed . . . managed to wrangle slots in Army Reserve and National Guard units. Of the many tragedies of Vietnam, this raw class discrimination strikes me as the most damaging to the ideal that all Americans are created equal and *owe equal allegiance* to their country."[12] If you are among the many who think that Powell is a good man fallen among thieves, this should reinforce your impressions.

On the other hand, like so many in the U.S. officer corps, Colin Powell seems to combine strong general principles with

a very particular and refined application of them: the reverse
of *ad hominem* in fact, since they apply to everyone except the
most prominent person for whom raw class discrimination
was an overwhelming determining factor.

In any case, for Bush the Younger, despite his occasional
and contradictory bluster, the possibility of transfer to
Indochina was infinitesimal, since the F-102, the Delta
Dagger, that his connections had placed him into training
with, was being phased out, and was not used in Vietnam.
Indeed, the air force had ordered all overseas F-102 'Delta
Dagger' units closed by June 30, 1970.

Frankly, had it been Bill Clinton, we may have suspected
ostentatious preemptive ass-covering here in Bush's choice of
unit, but nothing in George W. Bush's record so far in his life
gave any great signs of such political foresight, rather a
feeling of invulnerability and entitlement. But where there's a
will there's a way. He *could* have transferred to a unit with
more up-to-date planes, or even to the regular air force if he
could not control his berserker warrior urges. He didn't.

Moreover Bush's campaign has even used his training on
the obsolete plane to justify his early discharge, almost a year
before his scheduled discharge, since other F-102 pilots were
also being released early. But they can't answer the obvious
question—why spend so much money to train a National
Guardsman for two years on a plane that was already being
phased out?

Self-confessed Bush supporter and former commander of
the Texas ANG Major General Bobby W. Hodges told the
Boston Globe that the F-102 was still flying a year after Bush

left the service. If he "had come back to Houston, I would
have kept him flying the 102 until he got out, but I don't recall
him coming back at all," he said.[13]

That tick on the box for no overseas service obviously exer-
cised Bush's spin doctors since even the most geographically
challenged Texan knows that Vietnam is overseas. They have
been in a spin every time it surfaces. They have not yet
claimed that the dog ate his application, but they have indeed
come very close. Quantum particles can apparently be in two
different places at the same time. And so, it would appear was
George W. Bush's heart, which indeterminately yearned to be
in Vietnam—and safe at home in Texas at the same time.

After the *Washington Post* tasked him with the tick, the
White House provided a statement from a former state-level
air guard personnel officer, excusing the president on the
grounds that since he "was applying for a specific position
with the 147th Fighter Group, it would have been inappropriate for him to have volunteered for an overseas assignment, and he probably was so advised by the military
personnel clerk assisting him in completing the form."

Later in another interview, the spotty memory syndrome
resurfaced. He claimed to the *Washington Post* that "had my
unit been called up, I'd have gone (to Vietnam). I was prepared
to go." Indeed, in total contradiction to his confessions to Texan
newspapers while he was running for governor, he has claimed
that as he was finishing his flight training at the end of 1970,
he "tried to volunteer" for overseas duty in the Palace Alert
program which sent F-102 pilots abroad, "occasionally to
Vietnam." "I did ask and I was told, 'You're not going.'" In *A*

Charge to Keep he says that he and his friend, Fred Bradley, talked to Lt. Col. Killian about it, but he told them "the program was being phased out, that a few more pilots would go, but that Fred and I had not logged enough flight hours to participate."[14] Bradley also backed up the story.

In fact, the Palace Alert program wound up a week after Bush finished flight school, which adds extra suspicion about his narrative. If we assume that his buddy Bradley's convenient and expediently recalled story is indeed the truth, the whole truth, and nothing but the truth, it leads to some interesting questions. If Bush wanted to go to Vietnam, despite pulling strings to get into the guard, despite training on an aircraft being phased out of overseas service, and despite ticking the "no" box for overseas service, there were much more effective ways to do so than signing up for a program like Palace Alert.

But, then that would mean he lied to those Texan papers when he admitted that it was flying with the guard—or Vietnam. Indeed, it also meant he lied when NBC's Tim Russert asked him point-blank on *Meet the Press*, "Were you in favor of the war in Vietnam?" Bush answered, "I supported my government. I did. And would have gone had my unit been called up, by the way." So Russert clarified, "But you didn't volunteer or enlist to go." Afflicted with a memory loss of his tales of trying to go with the Palace Alert program, the Bush the Younger replied, "No, I didn't. You're right. I served, I flew fighters and enjoyed it and we provided a service for our country."[15]

But someone forgot to hand out the revised hymn sheets

since, only two weeks afterward, his campaign chairman, Marc Racicot, repeated that Bush "signed up for dangerous duty. He volunteered to go to Vietnam. He wasn't selected to go, but nonetheless served his country very well."[16]

When Governor Bush was launching himself toward the White House, the *Washington Post* went to Craig Stapleton, described as a long-standing friend and married to Bush's cousin, for an explanation and exoneration of his buddy's behavior. "All of a sudden everybody moves and you're still standing in the center. He didn't dodge the military, But he didn't volunteer to go to Vietnam and get killed either,"[17] Stapleton vouchsafed in words almost certainly cleared with the campaign beforehand.

It is interesting years afterwards to look back and see Bush cast as a centrist. One has to think hard to remember that he had passed as a "compassionate" moderate conservative for the purposes of election—in pretty much the same cynical way he is now posing as a veteran, one supposes.

However, we have no reason to doubt that Stapleton was speaking with the candidate's blessing. He was a partner with Bush in Texas Rangers baseball team, and a major fund-raiser for the presidential campaign. He is now the politically appointed U.S. ambassador in Prague, where local politicians say he does not bother consulting the State Department, but calls up George directly when he thinks something needs doing—such as browbeating the Czechs into joining the "coalition."

So in the end, when the wiggling had to stop, Bush the Younger declared, "I served, and I am proud of my service.

Yet I know it was nothing comparable to what our soldiers and pilots were doing in battle in Vietnam. I lost several friends there, pilots I trained with in flight school. They are heroes."[18]

As we have seen, "served" is a buzzword he uses a lot. Bush himself had preemptively softened up Russert by declaring, "What I don't like is when people say serving in the guard . . . may not be a true service." Of course it *may* indeed be a true service, as the poor mailmen in the National Guard now sweating it out in the Sunni triangle on extended terms *may* testify. But it *may* also have been a way of dodging *hazardous* service, as so many accuse the president of doing.

However, those carefully chosen words, representing the administration as the friend of National Guardsmen, and slandering critics of *his* service as detractors of *theirs*, echoed across the GOP amplifiers. Congressman Darell Issa, the man behind Arnold Schwarzenegger's recall and election campaigns in California, happily attacked Democrats for impugning the patriotism of *all* National Guardsmen, while South Carolina Governor Mark Sanford asserted that they were "taking shots" at the president for "being a guardsman."

So it was when he was running for the presidency that the pattern developed, what one might call genuine signs of military talent. Danton called for *"De l'audace, et encore de l'audace et toujours de l'audace!"* (Bravery, again bravery, and all the time, bravery!) Bush and his team have been pretty audacious in their counterattack. While the president has wrapped himself in the purloined flag and uniform of a veteran, he and his followers have impugned the patriotism and service of genuine veterans like John Kerry, and most extraordinarily, succeeded in ousting Senator Max Cleland, a triple-amputee war veteran on the grounds of his alleged lack of patriotism.

When it comes to questions about the questionable record of the young George W. Bush, or exploration of the numerous contradictions and inconsistencies in the stories that he and his entourage have spun, it is "gutter politics," say those wonderful people who hounded Clinton and gave a waiting world Willy Horton attack ads.

8 OLD MONEY

WHAT FORMER TEXAS GOVERNOR Ann Richards said so memorably of Bush Sr., applies with even more strength to George W. Bush. He was born with a silver foot in his mouth, combining the strengths of Old Money, Ivy League, Northeastern origins—the closest that America has to an aristocracy—with the Texas oil cabal.

This unfortunate conjunction has combined the Old Money's self-assurance to the point of arrogance, its sense of absolute entitlement, with the brashness and avaricious insouciance of the nouveau riche—and *their* sense of entitlement. In the East, you were rich because of family. In the South, you were rich because God loved you, personally. In the process of recombining social memes in Bush the Younger, this seems to have stripped out any of the sense of noblesse oblige of the Old Money in favor of a doubled meme for a sense of entitlement.

In his way very astute, Bush Sr. moved from Yale to Texas. From a geographical and political point of view, perhaps we could see this as a prescient recognition from some of the old East Coast Republican elite that in the long term, not only was Abraham Lincoln dead, but the Confederacy had won. Bush the Elder was already there, in place, with his family when the old Southern Democrats became Republicans, and consolidated their control of Washington.

In its own way Bush the Younger's repeated invocation in his autohagiography of "faith, family, and friends," is an unconscious echo of Margaret Thatcher's famous declaration, "There's no such thing as society. There are individual men and women, and there are families." Surprisingly, while Thatcher's statement is much quoted against her as epitomizing rampant selfishness masquerading as a political philosophy, Bush the Younger's equivalent has met with enough approbation to be the theme of his TV-campaign ads. It maybe the addition of "faith" that koshers it for Americans, and since his conversion, the faith thing has indeed moved electoral mountains for him, particularly in the Bible Belt, while the family and friends had always come up trumps before and continue to do so.[19]

Apart from his, apparently self-evident, advantages of being an Ivy League graduate, the referees George W. Bush put on his Air National Guard application show how well embedded the Bush dynasty had become in the Lone Star State's elite. He cited Blaine P. Kerr, who became a top executive of Pennzoil, and C. Fred Chambers, a Texas oilman who was so close to the Bushes that they later named one of their dogs after him. Since Bush Sr. described him as "one of my best friends" when he died, we must presume this was a compliment.

The third referee was James L. Bayless, a Texas lobbyist and lawyer who proves that what goes around comes around. He began as legislative Counsel to Senator John Tower and was Ronald Reagan's "Associate Director of the Office of Presidential Personnel." And then he was advisor to Bush Sr.'s Presidential Transition Team. The University of Texas has a James L. Bayless professorship of Free Enterprise, which about sums it up in the state that gave the world Enron and the S&L scandal.

But the Texas elite's pride in being self-made, however ill-founded it was in view of the chronic croneyism and prevalent porkbarreling that enriched them, seems to have persuaded them that they did not owe anything to society at large, but rather to the mutual back-scratching with those who had helped them along.

In contrast, in the old days, the scions of Old Money lined up to do their duty. They knew that they had earned their wealth the most difficult way—by inheriting it. Their notion of aristocracy often did carry with it a sense of obligation to match the privilege. There were Teddy Roosevelt's Rough Riders, in the last days of the cavalry, who volunteered to take up the white man's burden in the Spanish-American War. Roosevelt, for all his bumptiousness, his massive ego, and genuine courage, was the opposite of the modern Republican.

As has been pointed out, it takes the characteristic inbred brainlessness of the aristocrat to think that there's something inherently superior about riding larger, vulnerable, and highly visible horses in formation towards infantry with rapid firing guns. The machine gun's effect was eventually sharp enough to penetrate the mind even of the most effete aristocrat, even if took a whole half a millennium after Agincourt to do so thoroughly.

As a result, by the First World War, the Lafayette Escadrille fighter squadron was filled with young preppies and Ivy Leaguers so eager to do their bit that they volunteered to fight for the French even before the technical detail of U.S. entry into the war had actually been resolved. Fighter pilots had a personalized chivalrous glamour denied the poor bloody infantry in the trenches, lined up for wholesale plebeian mayhem and butchery.

Even so, by the time of Vietnam, being a fighter pilot retained some of its upper-class charm—hence the exclusiveness of the 111th. But instead of jousting one-on-one with the Red Baron, in the skies over Flanders, times had changed. A quick, anonymous, and very fast, surface-to-air missile was as likely to be a pilot's ticket to Valhalla as a duel in the sky.

So the modern knights of the 147th Fighter Wing 111th Fighter Squadron of the Texas Air National Guard, were perverse by earlier standards of chivalry. As they feasted around their round table, their implicit pledge was never to go on any perilous quest, simply to joust around their home base, secure from any Vietcong giants or dragons who may have challenged them. Later, as preparations for Afghanistan went on, the warrior-pretender President Bush was to refer approvingly to the *Puff the Magic Dragon*, the AC130 gunship with heavy fire power. He told the cabinet that during Vietnam, it "was way more effective than a Northern Alliance cavalry. It is a lethal weapon. My reaction was, if you've got a shot at the enemy, take it in any way you can."[20] But of course, despite this tough-boy talk, he had made sure that he had had no first hand experience of the beast.

With the ambivalence of American political tradition, poor little rich boys like the Bush sprigs faced problems in an American society where it is indeed assumed that they must be effete scions, pampered and spoon-fed, rather than the self-made American ideal that justifies plutocracy as a reward for hard work. The electoral demands for "log cabin to White House" back-stories for the politically ambitious impelled the rush to prove themselves by the Roosevelts, the Kennedys, etc., to show that, even with the profound disadvantages of trust funds, an Ivy League education, and silver spoons in their mouths, they would have made it on their own.

War has often been a quick solution for expunging the hereditary wimpish image—as the iconography of John F. Kennedy and his wartime exploits with *PT-109* showed. But an acceptable longer-term alternative was to show that they could have made it as self-made businesspeople and entrepreneurs even without Old Money and the social safety net bequeathed them. The process was an old one: In the early nineteenth century when asked why Harrow, the English public school, endowed by a pious philanthropist to educate poor scholars, had so many rich pupils, its headmaster hastily pointed that the children had no money—it was their parents who were rich. This stratagem was a favorite for the establishment of the proper *bona fides* of, for example, twigs off the Bush dynasty.

Indeed, George Bush Sr. tried a form of it. As well as genuinely volunteering for war at the earliest opportunity, he tried to reinvent himself as a Texas oil baron afterward. He later declared, "They say I'm a patrician. I don't know what the word means. I'll have to look it up." This dumbed-down act is reminiscent of the Etonians in Britain who attempted nasal Liverpool accents in emulation of the Beatles back when a working class hero was something to be. While with Bush Sr., it was indeed an act, his son seems to have carried the "Method school of drama" to extremes. There is some serious suspicion that he may actually be as socially dumb and naive as he pretends and he certainly lacks the easy charm that the Old Money brigade used to camouflage their power and wealth. He has tried so hard to become a Texan oil millionaire that he has almost become a parody of one. While we can forgive him supporting "bidness," as any Texan pol would, you don't have to be snobbish to worry a little when the president thinks he has a finger on the "nucular" trigger.

In his parody of self-madeness, he has concocted several self-made business disasters from which his social network has rescued him, and during his college day he seems to have sublimated any military urges into a frenzy of Texas-style jockishness with rugby, football, baseball, and basketball, the Armour Council. But then came the coolest role of all—George W. Bush, ace jet fighter pilot ("naval aviator" was, of course, then in another ocean and another century).

Bush the Younger is certainly no coward in the physical

sense, but we can deduce from his own candid comments to the Texas media while running for governor and from the statements of his social cohorts that his generation and milieu felt that actual war was beneath them, that they had higher and better things to do with their time.

In some ways, the description that William Eckhardt wrote of ROTC students at the University of California, back in 1968 could pass as a pen portrait of Bush the Younger. The cadets, he found:

> compared with student draft resisters were found to have experienced strict childhood discipline in relation to a dominant father figure. They showed a strong concern about proving for their masculinity, used more alcohol, felt powerless to influence their country's actions, felt troubled about their sexual inadequacy, defined independence as loss of self-control, preferred a well-ordered and structured environment, admitted being self-centred and egotistical, felt shy with girls but boasted to their fellows of their sexual conquests, claimed little real intimacy with and poor relationships with the opposite sex, admitted treating females as objects, tended to seek dominance-submission relationships and were relatively aggressive, impulsive, irresponsible, and non-intellectual with a poorly developed conscience.[21]

George W. Bush would certainly have been at home in the

ROTC—but in a case of delayed development, he waited until he was in the guard to live down to this description.

His colleagues say that he was a good pilot, and he himself in *A Charge to Keep* says that he, "continued flying with my unit for the next several years."[22] He does not mention his later mysterious abstinence from a pursuit that by all accounts he enjoyed so much—all the more so, one suspects, since it kept him at the opposite end of the world from people who may have been trying to shoot him down.

In some ways, like Ronald Reagan who had persuaded himself that his war service with the U.S. Army Air Force making training films and heroic war movies in Los Angeles actually saw him abroad liberating death camps, Bush the Younger does now seem to have persuaded himself that he was indeed a veteran. Indeed, emulating Humpty Dumpty, when he uses a word, it means just what he chooses it to mean, neither more nor less, so we can agree with his oft repeated claim that he "served" during the Vietnam War. But not in it.

Taking all the evidence, and his own statements, even through the fog of politics, it is clear and irrefutable that George W. Bush used his social and family networks, and indeed, if you count Skull and Bones as a cult, his faith-based networks, to ensure that he did not engage in actual combat in the "war of his generation." He had no sense of noblesse oblige, and no sense of shame about it. That sense of entitlement, God-given obligation, and free privilege for the rich can, of course, without too much scrutiny, be discerned in his politics.

9 ODIOUS COMPARISONS

OF COURSE, BEING A genuine, rather than an adoptive, son of the hookworm and pellagra belt like George W. Bush, Bill Clinton was well aware of the potential effect of evasion on a political career for someone who had chosen his parents as unwisely as the kid from Hope.

The Republicans used Clinton's wrigglings over the draft to great effect, with the barefaced hypocrisy and assiduity we have come to know so well—but even so still have to gasp at in admiration. It is instructive to look at what Clinton actually did, which despite its classically Clintonesque contortions between integrity and self interest, was eventually the right thing.

Having originally secured a notional ROTC berth that would protect him from the draft, Clinton cannily anticipated the political effects of this down the line: which Bush, Quayle, and Cheney did not. Or maybe it was canniness all around and all parties really knew that a blue-blood Republican would be excused behavior that would condemn a Democrat son of the soil.

It seems that Clinton did indeed call on the aid of Senator James Fulbright and others to help defer him from the draft, including a commitment to join the ROTC at the University of Arkansas.

In any case, Clinton dropped out of the ROTC and put his name in for the draft—and doubtless knew that he had done the right thing because the Deity ensured that he drew a number highly unlikely to be called. But he felt guilty because he may have misled Colonel Eugene Holmes, the commander of the ROTC unit at the University of Arkansas, who had worked hard to ensure his acceptance. Clinton wrote him a letter that the GOP dirty-tricks department, naturally, unearthed and publicized as the New Hampshire primaries approached.

It is instructive that the soul-searching, albeit occasionally self-serving letter was circulated widely by the right-wingers all over the Internet. It is here quoted at length, to fill a vacuum. At no point in his career, from cheerleader at Andover, throughout his service in the National Guard, to his present role as commander in chief, has George W. Bush shown anything like the sensitivity or self-awareness, let alone the self-criticism, of Clinton on this issue. It explores the issues that haunted many young Americans at the time. There is no evidence whatsoever that George W. Bush had any doubt that his route to avoid service in Vietnam was simply a legitimate exercise of his birthright.

Dear Colonel Holmes,

I am sorry to be so long in writing. I know I had promised to let you hear from me at least once a month, and from now on you will, but I've had to have some time to think about this first letter. Almost daily since my return to England I have thought about writing, about what I want to and ought to say.

First, I want to thank you, not just for saving me from the draft, but for being so kind and decent to me last summer, when I was as low as I have ever been. One thing that made the bond we struck in good faith somewhat palatable to me was my high regard for you personally. In retrospect, it seems that the admiration might not have been mutual had you known a little more about me, about my political beliefs and activities. At least you might have thought I was more fit for the draft than for ROTC.

Let me try to explain. As you know, I worked for two years in a very minor position on the Senate Foreign Relations Committee. I did it for the experience and the salary but also for the opportunity, however small, of working every day against a war I opposed and despised with a depth of feeling I had observed solely for racism in America before Vietnam. I did not take the matter lightly but studied it carefully, and there was a time when not many people had more information about Vietnam at hand than I did. I have written and spoken and

marched against the war. One of the national
organizers of the Vietnam Moratorium is a close
friend of mine. After I left Arkansas last summer,
I went to Washington to work in the national
headquarters of the Moratorium, then to England
to organize the Americans here for the demonstrations October 15 and November 16.

Interlocked with the war is the draft issue,
which I did not begin to consider separately until
early 1968. For a law seminar at Georgetown I
wrote a paper on the legal arguments for and
against allowing, within the Selective Service
System, the classification of selective conscientious
objection, for those opposed to participation in a
particular war, not simply to 'participation in war
in any form.'

From my work I came to believe that the draft
system itself is illegitimate. No government really
rooted in limited, parliamentary democracy should
have the power to make its citizens fight and kill
and die in a war they may oppose, a war which even
possibly may be wrong, a war which, in any case,
does not involve immediately the peace and
freedom of the nation.

The draft was justified in WWII because the life
of the people collectively was at stake. Individuals
had to fight, if the nation was to survive, for the lives
of their countrymen and their way of life. Vietnam
is no such case. Nor was Korea an example, where,

in my opinion, certain military action was justified but the draft was not, for the reasons stated above.

Because of my opposition to the draft and the war, I am in great sympathy with those who are not willing to fight, kill, and maybe die for their country (i.e the particular policy of a particular government) right or wrong. Two of my friends at Oxford are conscientious objectors. I wrote a letter of commendation for one of them to his Mississippi draft board, a letter which I am more proud of than anything I wrote at Oxford last year. One of my roommates is a draft resister who is possibly under indictment and may never be able to go home again. He is one of the bravest, best men I know. That he is considered a criminal is an obscenity.

The decision not to be a resister and then the related subsequent decisions were the most difficult of my life. I decided to accept the draft in spite of my beliefs for one reason: to maintain my political viability within the system. For years I have worked to prepare myself for a political life characterized by both practical political ability and concern for rapid social progress. It is a life I still feel compelled to try to lead. I do not think our system of government is by definition corrupt, however dangerous and inadequate it has been in recent years. (The society may be corrupt, but that is not the same thing, and if that is true we are all finished anyway.)

When the draft came, despite political convictions, I was having a hard time facing the prospect of fighting a war I had been fighting against, and that is why I contacted you. ROTC was the one way left in which I could possibly, but not positively, avoid both Vietnam and resistance. Going on with my education, even coming back to England, played no part in my decision to join ROTC. I am back here, and would have been at Arkansas Law School because there is nothing else I can do. In fact, I would like to have been able to take a year out perhaps to teach in a small college or work on some community action program and in the process decide whether to attend law school or graduate school and how to begin putting what I have learned to use.

But the particulars of my personal life are not nearly as important to me as the principles involved. After I signed the ROTC letter of intent I began to wonder whether the compromise I had made with myself was not more objectionable than the draft would have been, because I had no interest in the ROTC program in itself and all I seem to have done was to protect myself from physical harm. Also, I began to think I had deceived you, not by lies because there were none but by failing to tell you all the things I'm writing now. I doubt that I had the mental coherence to articulate them then.

At that time, after we had made our agreement

and you had sent my 1-D deferment to my draft board, the anguish and loss of my self-regard and self-confidence really set in. I hardly slept for weeks and kept going by eating compulsively and reading until exhaustion brought sleep. Finally, on September 12 I stayed up all night writing a letter to the chairman of my draft board saying basically what is in the last paragraph, thanking him for trying to help in a case where he really couldn't, and stating that I couldn't do the ROTC after all and would he please draft me as soon as possible.

I never mailed the letter, but I did carry it on me every day until I got on the plane to return to England. I didn't mail the letter because I didn't see, in the end, how my going in the army and maybe going to Vietnam would achieve anything except a feeling that I had punished myself and gotten what I deserved. So I came back to England to try to make something of this second year of my Rhodes scholarship.

And that is where I am now, writing to you because you have been good to me and have a right to know what I think and feel. I am writing too in the hope that my telling this one story will help you to understand more clearly how so many fine people have come to find themselves still loving their country but loathing the military, to which you and other good men have devoted years, lifetimes, of the best service you could give. To many of us, it is no longer clear what is service and what is disservice, or if it is clear, the conclusion is likely to be illegal.

Forgive the length of this letter. There was much to say. There is still a lot to be said, but it can wait. Please say hello to Col. Jones for me.

Merry Christmas.

Sincerely,
Bill Clinton

Since he had mentioned his part in the increasingly large demonstrations in Britain against the war in Vietnam (I should perhaps declare an interest: I helped organize contingents from Liverpool for them as well, but do not recollect ever meeting the future president.). This frank exposition of the very real career quandary that William J. Clinton faced, leads us to the question of why another contemporary, George W. Bush, also seemingly earmarked for a political career, could be so confident, indeed arrogant, to assume that there would be no consequences for him?

When Clinton's letter was leaked, Ted Koppel[23] on *Nightline* charged him, "Governor Clinton, this is not 1969, it's not 1978. You are now running, among other things, for the post of commander in chief of the United States, and while legally, technically, in every respect everything you say may be quite accurate, you know this letter has a flavor which is not going to sit well with folks down South, in particular, folks from Arkansas, among other places."

Clinton astutely replied, tying others' behavior to his, and in some ways providing appropriate commentary on what would later be revealed about young George Bush, "I said Dan Quayle ought to just tell the truth, get the facts out and let it go, you know. He was for the Vietnam War, but got into the National Guard. That wasn't an option for me. They were all full, all those slots. I was against the Vietnam War, but I gave up a deferment and put myself back into the draft. I got a high lottery number. If the people know the facts, I think they'll be all right."

If this was such a big issue in the Clinton election, why had Dubya's dubious war record not come up earlier? In fact, it had, in the gubernatorial elections. However, as we saw, the Democrats had not campaigned with the ferocity that would have made a difference because lots of Democratic power brokers had used exactly the same method, and there was a certain bipartisanship in Texas politics.

After all, it was pretty much the same white, Anglo Southern oligarchy running both parties, and there was a lot of mutual back-scratching. It would have been hard to attack Bush, without getting blowback on Bentsen and Barnes, since he was a Democrat when he pulled the necessary strings for Bush. However, the modern GOP would not recognize a quid if a pro quoth it at them.

10 THE MILITARY TRADITION

FOR OUTSIDERS, THIS AMERICAN delving into military careers, or lack of them, is peculiar and idiosyncratic, almost as bizarre as the search for sexual peccadilloes that usually now accompanies American elections. In other countries, veterans who play upon their service are regarded as boring at best and ridiculous at worst, but if they intrude their military pedigree into politics, it is somehow also dangerous and distasteful.

Perhaps the clearest exposition of the transatlantic difference was Paddy Ashdown, the former leader of the British Liberal Democrats. Although he got very little electoral leverage for being a veteran of and captain in Special Boat Service, Britain's elite Marine Commando unit, his poll ratings shot up when he replied "yes" when the yellow press asked him if he was having a love affair with his secretary.

Even so, if there is one thing worse than having a military career and flaunting it—it is *pretending* to have one and flaunting it while sending other people to die. Most of the democratic world would agree with French Nobel Literature Prize–winner Romain Rolland, who at the outbreak of the First World War, said somewhat more pithily and memorably than his more usual ten-volume line in novels: "I find war detestable. But even more detestable are those who praise war without participating in it."

Certainly, while his comment fits George W. Bush to a T, Rolland would find slim pickings for a novel in the president's military career. Bush the Younger's entirely spurious patina of a soldier and veteran covers a hollow shell of dodging fighting but active campaigning for politicians who were instrumental in prolonging the war, and authorizing a draft that ensured that citizens who had chosen their parents unwisely were torn from their desks and workbenches and dropped to meet their fate in muddy jungles at the other end of the world.

We can admit that revulsion against the military after Vietnam was perhaps the predominant left and liberal emotion. In many ways, we blamed the victims, the ones who could not escape the draft. We saw an army of William Calleys, but forgot that the massacre at My Lai was stopped by an army pilot, Warrant Officer Hugh Thompson, who landed his helicopter and ordered his door gunner Lawrence Colburn, to shoot the GIs if necessary to stop the killing. Admittedly, it took thirty years to get them the Soldier's Medal they deserved from the government, but they were hardly icons of the liberal left for that period, during which they represented a military tradition equally as strong as Calleys—but ignored.

Now the pendulum has swung to the other extreme. To

criticize any aspect of the military is a form of thought-crime. One can hardly see Bush and Rumsfeld giving medals to ethical heroes like Thompson, but throughout American society it has become increasingly difficult to question anything the Pentagon or military is doing. In the present climate it is difficult to envisage a television network brave enough to make a program like *Sergeant Bilko*, let alone *M.A.S.H.*, for fear of being accused of disloyalty.

Of course, as we have said, the commander in chief, by wrapping himself in a flamboyant combination of the flag and the uniform has assumed a form of papal infallibility which protects him from any questioning of his past, present, or future roles.

The United States needs more little drummer boys pointing out that the president has no clothes, regardless of the military gear he wears. Indeed that would be in the mainstream of the British and American traditions that have always tended to at once mock and fear the pretensions of the military.

For example, James Madison in his 1799 *Political Reflections* described two "momentous truths" in politics: "First. That the fetters imposed on liberty at home have ever been forged out of the weapons provided for defense against real, pretended, or imaginary dangers from abroad. Secondly. That there never was a people whose liberties long survived a standing army." One cannot help wondering whether Karl Rove and Bush the Younger may not have read this and taken it as more in the nature of sound political advice than a principled warning!

Unfashionable though it may be to question the founding father's wisdom, insofar as he was right on this issue, it was for the wrong reasons. While Madison was entirely right in his first momentous truth: pretended dangers from abroad have indeed often been the occasion for severe and unconstitutional repression in the United States, he was incorrect in his premonition of how the armed forces would be used.

While the founders envisaged unscrupulous monarchs, chief executives, or generals using the army to seize power, it is not so much the actual army, but its *prestige* that the modern day putschists abuse. They themselves are what Christopher Hitchens calls the "braver sort of Pentagon intellectuals," who are too cerebral to wave flags but quite happy to encourage the habit in others, and their comrades in the White House, such as Dick Cheney and his entourage, not to mention the civilian in chief himself, George W. Bush. Between them, in the name of those hyped-up external dangers they have made it almost blasphemous to question the finance, purpose, or conduct of the armed forces.

The development of American deference to the professional army is a strange and recent phenomenon. For the greatest part of the history of the Republic, the standing army was small, and the militia so celebrated by the NRA in the second amendment were an inebriated joke. As Washington wrote to Congress, (September 24, 1776) "To place any dependence upon the militia is assuredly resting upon a broken staff."[24] The militia is, of course, the lineal ancestor of the National Guard.

The original idea of all able bodied men being mustered for defense went back to Anglo-Saxon times in England, but fell apart by the nineteenth century, eroded by the absence of

a existential military threat to either the American states or to
the British islands. Also, in both places, the growing social
separation in the nineteenth century led to the local elites
forming what were much more exclusive, semi-private
militia companies.

In the U.S., the gap between natives and immigrants exac-
erbated that social separation. Somewhat snobbish, with enlistment by invitation only, these units had no expectation of being
called up to fight overseas, let alone on the frontier with the
Indians. They were to keep the lesser breeds who were arriving
on these shores within the law, not to bear the white man's
burden later, which is why the various armories in New York
are built like fortresses. They *were* fortresses, and served the
same purpose as forts on Indian reservations, to keep the locals
pacified. They paved the way for units like the Texas Air
National Guard, for young Yalies like Bush the Younger.

But even while the private militia were local powerhouses
for social and political networks, almost like suburban volunteer fire companies, general respect for the professional soldiery was not much above that given by the Duke of
Wellington, who famously called the troops who won the
Battle of Waterloo for him, "the scum of the earth."

Americans shared the feeling of many British "that it was
disgrace to a family for one of its members to go for a soldier."
As Corelli Barnet said, "Although the gradual reform of conditions of army life and discipline has put an end to a rank
and file of felons, drunks, and pathological outcasts, the army
was still recruited mostly from the very poorest and most
ignorant. The army was, in a real sense, the only welfare

service provided by the British state for the rescue of such unfortunates."[25] Indeed, a similar argument has been made for the present U.S. Army, the only part of the U.S. population outside the membership of Congress that enjoys the benefits of a welfare state and free health care.

The old Republican ethos, once again drawing upon strong British traditions, regarded the standing army as a threat to liberty. Jefferson reinforced Madison's warnings, saying, "The spirit of this country is totally adverse to a large military force"[26] and echoing common British Whig prejudice he calculated that "a naval force can never endanger our liberties, nor occasion bloodshed, a land force would do both."[27]

Walt Whitman's service in the Civil War Army led him to distrust the military as an institution representing privilege. "The whole present system of the officering and personnel of the Army and Navy of these States, and the spirit and letter of their trebly-aristocratic rules and regulations, is a monstrous exotic, a nuisance and a revolt, and belongs here just as much as orders of nobility or the Pope's council of cardinals. I say that if the present theory of our army and navy is possible and true, then rest of America is an unmitigated fraud."[28]

The key instrument that the British Parliament used to ensure that the king did not try to rule without it was the need to pass the Mutiny Act every year, which alone preserved military discipline. (In contrast, the king of France managed to put off summoning his equivalent for over a hundred years!) The British monarch may have been commander in chief of the armed forces, but it was only on an annual franchise from the legislature.

The Americans, while endowing their president with much of the prestige and power of a Hanoverian monarch, save for the tedium of facing reelection after four years, omitted this useful check on his position. If Congress were not so supine now, it would be a useful tradition to reestablish in the face of overweening executive authority, but that's another story.

Instructively, the entire U.S. standing army in 1941 was not much larger than the garisson in Iraq on the 40th anniversary of the D-Day landings. The maintenance of conscription for so many years after the Second World War, the presence of real threats in the world, meant the hugely expanded military that developed in that war never shrank back in size or prestige. Sadly, it appears that American society is poorly equipped to deal with the military and its role, if the way that Congress rolls over when the military appropriations come up is any guide. Perhaps it is the low public regard for politicians and public servants that seeks people to seek virtue in at least one arm of the state.

However, the prominence of the military in politics and decision making is also a reflection of a shift in the regional balance of power in the United States as the Confederacy strikes back. We can regard the election of Bush the Younger and the religious right to power as Robert E. Lee's revenge.

There is more behind Bush's disturbing militarism than an attempt to cover up draft dodging and privileged "skiving." There is also his desperate attempt to be accepted as a real Texan, a self-made man of action from the allegedly aristocratic Southern tradition rather than a pampered Ivy League brat who just happens to be in the Lone Star State.

The part of Texas that the Old Money, East Coast Bush stock grafted himself onto is the Southern end of the American folkway that includes Kentucky colonels and a militaristic tradition that measures manliness by military service. Those Federal military bases in the old Confederacy not only feed the local economies with federal funds, they also feed a Southern self-perception of Spartan-style military ethos, even if much of that tradition was based on local militias being ready to repress slave rebellions or hunt down runaways.

Of course, with almost 40 percent of the military now coming from ethnic groups that would probably not have been allowed to vote in the Confederacy, let alone bear arms, the ethos and the sordid reality of history do clash. What is more, they can easily be put in a long line of "heavily armed victims," like the Serb militias in Bosnia or Israeli settlers, people with an historical sense of victimhood who happen to be much stronger than those they claim are persecuting them. The ghosts of the lost Confederacy, the sense that they are looked down at inside the country, ally with a feeling that the U.S. has been getting kicked around by the rest of the world—and it's payback time. These are dangerous enough feelings in a street gang or a militia, but they are terrifying to discern in the administration of the world's only superpower.

But such people share with President Bush the Red Queen's ability to believe six impossible things before breakfast—and mutually contradictory ones to boot. The folkways that brought ethnic cleansing to the Indians, slavery to the South, and drove out the Mexicans are now in charge of the United States. And like Bush the Younger, they like uniforms.

11 ROLL ALABAMA ROLL

BUT WHERE DID THAT YEAR GO?

IN THE OLD DAYS, wars were fought during the campaigning season, summertime, when the fighting was easy, between sowing and harvest, while it was warm enough to fight and the cannon fodder would not be missed back at the farm. Hence Tom Paine's denunciation of the "summer soldiers and sunshine patriots," who missed getting chilblains in Valley Forge.

In contrast, for George W. Bush, summer soldier extraordinaire, the sun has always shone during his military career. His campaigning season was year-round, whenever and wherever across the Confederacy a family friend had need of help to secure political office.

You would also think that Bush the Young would boast in his memoirs about his truly historic and meteoric promotion record. After six weeks basic training, by the beginning of September 1968, he was deemed such an outstanding officer that he was made second lieutenant without the tedium and formality of attending officer training school.

Bush's rapid commission, despite a complete absence of previous ROTC or flight experience, not to mention his abysmal score on the pilot aptitude test, was as possible in the nepotistic world of the Texas Air National Guard as promotion to colonel in Kentucky. It is unlikely to have passed scrutiny in the USAF proper, where attendance at an officer training school would have been required. Some accounts, in fact, suggest it was an "historic" promotion, the only such except for flight surgeons and other desperately needed skills, where the rank, but not necessarily the military and command skills of an officer were necessary.

With his assured promotion, Second Lieutenant Bush took two months leave to go campaigning for Edward Gurney Jr., an old family friend in Florida, who had already been elected to Congress "based on opposition to communism abroad and creeping socialism in this country," but wanted to be derangedly right wing in the Senate as well.

With the help of Bush and Jim Allison he succeeded, and became the first Republican senator from Florida since the Reconstruction. But it was, of course, an empty achievement for the GOP in any ethical sense. It was not Abraham Lincoln's Republican Party any more, it was more Jefferson Davis's. Indeed, it was Barry Goldwater's.

During the campaign, Gurney was sending coded messages about his opponent, former Florida governor LeRoy Collins, one of the few Southern Democrats to break ranks with the segregationists. It was not so much that Gurney positioned himself as an overt opponent of the civil rights movement—more that he painted Collins as a strong supporter of it. Someone—the Gurney campaign denied it was them, of course—circulated pictures of Collins at the head of the freedom marchers in Selma. He was there at the request of President Johnson negotiating a peaceful outcome of the March with Martin Luther King Jr., but the pictures were intended to show him heading the march and the coded message was enough for Florida voters.

It was the young Bush's first lesson in hardball politics but one can only suspect he absorbed it. No one has ever suggested that the Bushes were racist: they had too much of the East Coast patrician about them for that. But in best Machiavellian style, they certainly knew an expedient vote-winning issue when they saw it.

In early 1974, a grand jury indicted Senator Gurney, a last-ditch defender of resigned Richard Nixon, on several counts of perjury, bribery, and conspiracy in connection with campaign fundraising, but he eventually got off after the jury deadlocked.

James L. Martin, a Florida conservative, remembers that Bush the Younger's part in the trip was arranged between Gurney and Bush Sr. Later he recalls letting Bush Jr. know about Gurney's death, and that "he wrote me to say that Ed Gurney was an outstanding senator and a great American." Gurney escapes mention in George W. Bush's memoirs.

Fresh from his triumph in protecting the South from internal subversion, Second Lieutenant Bush went in November 1968 to Moody Air Force Base in Valdosta,

Georgia, for flight training, where apparently he actually did
quite well as a pilot, despite his 25 percent on the aptitude test.
Although we can be fairly sure that it would have had to be a
brave officer who dissed him on his progress after Richard M.
Nixon sent a plane down to pick him up for a date with his
daughter Tricia,[29] his success as a pilot is, in its own perverse
way, a testament to affirmative action. His promoters could
argue that they had seen the personal potential in this candidate instead of just relying on numerical test scores and those
similar artificial advantages that private schools can give. But
just in case we get carried away, we should remember that, to
complete the web of influence and patronage, Congressman
George Bush, his father, gave the commencement speech for
the graduating pilots.

Indeed, his first solo flight was hymned by the PR office of
the unit, "George Walker Bush is one member of the younger
generation who doesn't get his kicks from pot, or hashish, or
speed. . . . As far as kicks are concerned, Lt. Bush gets his
from the roaring afterburner of the F-102." One cannot help
wondering about the significance of the omissions in that
press release. Did the drafter know something, since booze
and cocaine are conspicuously absent from the pilot's alternative kick list?

Despite the afterburner boost of a congressional parent and
the White House, it does seem that he genuinely enjoyed
flying and was indeed good at it. But who would say any different? For example, the *Washington Post* had an obliging
quote from old Yalie chum and Houston roommate, Don
Ensenat, that he had to do night flying and so "no booze

twenty-four hours before" and, of course, he never saw Bush use illegal drugs. In the first Bush administration, Ensenat was ambassador to the oil rich state of Brunei. In the second, he was chief of protocol at the State Department. The Bushes are loyal to their friends.

Perhaps it would not be too cynical to suggest that such thoughts were also in the mind of his commander in the Texas Air National Guard, Lt. Col. Jerry B. Killian, when in recommending young Bush for promotion to first lieutenant November 1970, he reported the former Andover cheerleader as "a dynamic outstanding young officer," and "a top notch fighter interceptor pilot," who was "mature beyond his age."

"Lieutenant Bush's skills far exceed his contemporaries," Killian additionally rhapsodized in recommending that Bush be promoted. "He is a natural leader whom his contemporaries look to for leadership. Lieutenant Bush is also a good follower with outstanding disciplinary traits and an impeccable military bearing."

In retrospect, one can only smile when he gushes on, "Lt. Bush possesses vast potential and should be promoted well ahead of his contemporaries." And, of course, he had good connections too. Not least of which was Killian, whom the young George described as a friend in his autobiography.

However, then something went wrong. Despite what seemed to be a genuinely productive time in Houston and in the Air National Guard, where he actually more than fulfilled his service obligations, and had taken promotion, he suddenly changed. In 1971, the *Houston Post* had mentioned "George Bush Jr." considering running for State Senate, so he was thinking politics in some form. While too busy to join the campaign in Vietnam, the expensively trained fighter pilot, then attached himself to the Senate campaign of Republican Winton Blount in Alabama. Canvassing alongside George W. Bush for Blount, who was postmaster general under Richard Nixon, was Barry Goldwater.

These were bright days for the Republican Party. Nationally, the Democratic Party had put itself on the side of desegregation and equal rights. The party of Abraham Lincoln was in the process of converting Southern Democrats to Republicans, and while it was careful not to espouse outright racism or segregation, it developed the use of coded messages that it now uses so successfully to present itself as the party of white Americans beleaguered by federal and state coddling of minorities. Jim Allison who had already deployed such tactics in Florida for Gurney, recycled them to use in Alabama, and called upon Bush Jr. to help.

American politics has always been a circus, but Bush was working with the people who made it more reminiscent of the Coliseum than Barnum and Bailey. Ruthless and immoral distortion of opponent's positions, taking risks with racial relations, attacks bordering on libel, were all becoming part of their repertoire.

However, incumbent Senator John Sparkman's coded messages worked better than Blount's. Southern Democrat Sparkman was no reforming antisegregationist Collins. His coded messages allowed him to persuade many white Alabamians that he was a bosom buddy of Governor George Wallace, and to get the black voters as well since he

DESERTER 97

was running for the party of Kennedy and LBJ. It may not have helped that Blount seems to have had a streak of decency as well, allegedly playing similar mediating role to Collins in the great standoff when Alabama Governor George Wallace threatened to block the doors in the face of LBJ's federal troops to keep black students out of white schools.

> Pentagon officials believe they have been unable to locate Bin Laden because he has found a place to hide out where:
>
> 1) it is easy to get in if you have money;
> 2) no one will recognize or remember you;
> 3) no one will realize you have disappeared;
> 4) no one keeps any records of your comings and goings; and
> 5) you have no obligations or responsibilities.
>
> Pentagon analysts are still puzzled, however, as to how Bin Laden found out about the Alabama Air National Guard in the first place.

One would, of course, hesitate to suggest a causal relationship, but Blount, forced back into commerce by his election defeat prospered while his relationship with the Bush family flourished. In the 1980s his company Blount International completed the world's largest fixed-price contract, $2 billion, for the King Saud University in Riyadh, Saudi Arabia.

After President Bush Sr. won the first war in Iraq, the company showed the way for Halliburton by "turning the lights back on" in Kuwait with contracts to repair its war-damaged infrastructure. The old man, now deceased, would be happy to know that his son's company is now subcontracting for Halliburton in Iraq.

Blount was more cultured than the average Southern politician, richly endowing the Alabama Shakespeare Festival, which takes place in the lavish Blount Cultural Park in Montgomery. We know it is important, because Vice President Dick Cheney, formerly CEO of Halliburton, turned up for the opening. Shortly after the Blount campaign, the Bush family was tied into the Republican web even more tightly, when Nixon invited Bush Sr. to chair the Republican National Committee.

However, for Bush the Younger to work on his part of the web, in Alabama, he had to cover his absence from essential duties in Texas, where the Air National Guard did actually fly patrols. At the end of May 1972, he tried for a posting to the 9921st Air Reserve at Maxwell Air Base in Alabama. His commanders in Texas rubber-stamped it, even though they thought it was a long shot to transfer a recently graduated pilot to a postal unit that had no actual planes.

They could cover all sorts in the Lone Star State, but a move to Alabama made it, in a way, a federal case. After all, the young Bush had not signed up in the Air National Guard just to keep white women safe on the streets. That was what the Alabama National Guard infantry was for, so he had to make some accommodation to continue his six-year commitment to the guard while enhancing the family's political connection.

In some ways, we should just put a blank page here—which would be a suitable comment on the lack of documentation for First Lieutenant Bush's service to his country in Alabama as the war raged in Vietnam.

Lt. Col. Reese Bricken, the 9921st commander at Maxwell, told the *Boston Globe* later, "We met just one weeknight a month. We were only a postal unit. We had no airplanes. We had no pilots. We had no nothing." Even Albert Lloyd Jr., a retired Air National Guard colonel from Texas who was helping the Bush campaign "clarify" the candidate's service, told the *Globe* he was mystified why Bush's superiors at the time would approve duty at such a unit. He should know. He was personnel director of the Texas Air National Guard from 1969 to 1995.

There is a delicious sense of historical irony. There are postal workers now in the National Guard under commander in chief George W. Bush, who are risking their lives in Iraq, although their president once tried to switch from being a pilot to a glorified mailman with a pilot's license.

The Texas end of the guard had crossed their fingers and approved the transfer in May, but then the national command refused to ratify it and wrote to all concerned to tell them so at the end of July. In any case, Bush has never even claimed that he had tried to join the mailmen at Maxwell.

In the meantime, he had been summoned for his annual medical examination, which was due within one month of his July 6 birthday. This was essential if he wanted to keep on flying. Indeed, it was essential anyway, since, regardless of what he wanted, the air force, having spent a million on his training wanted him to carry on flying. He did not attend. Ever.

In September, by which time he had already been in Alabama for four months, his application was approved to

transfer to Alabama's 187th TAC Recon Group at Dannelly
Air Force Base for three months.

In a September 15 order he was commanded to report
to the 187th's commander, Lt. Col. William Turnipseed, "to
perform equivalent training." But neither the commander
nor his then administrative officer, Kenneth Lott, have any
recollection of Bush showing up. "Had he reported in, I
would have had some recall, and I do not," said
Turnipseed. "I had been in Texas, done my flight training
there. If we had had a first lieutenant from Texas, I would
have remembered."

Bush apparently remembers General Turnipseed,
according to his beleagured spokesman Dan Bartlett, who
was struggling to be an effective ventriloquist's dummy even
though the ventriloquist kept changing his lines. In fact,
Associated Press had reported four years before in 2000 that
Bush had said, "I read the comments from the guy who said
he doesn't remember me being there, but I remember being
there." And if Lt. Col. Turnipseed had been addressed so dis-
respectfully as "the guy" by the future commander in chief,
we can be sure that he would have remembered him, too.

He was also ordered to turn up for a medical examination.
Since then the excuses have rolled in—he was in Alabama,
and would have had to go to Texas. His plane was obsolete.

But Bush's memory is worth a Ph.D. to a psychology graduate. He also told the *Birmingham News* in 2000, "I can't
remember what I did, but I wasn't flying because they didn't
have the same airplane. I fulfilled my obligation to my
country."[30] By February 2, 2004, Bartlett said that Bush

"specifically remembers" performing some of his duties. But it seems that "specifically" means something different in Bush-speak, although Bartlett amusingly admitted that the first lieutenant's "irregular civilian work schedule could put strains on when he served, when he performed his duty." [31]

But having found out where their missing in inaction pilot was, the air force followed up with another order, dated September 29, 1972. This is among the documents released by the White House, and says that Bush had been suspended from flying for his failure to take the examination, which he should have gone to within a month of July 6.

It ordered him to comply with paragraph 2-10, AFM 35-13, which requires him to acknowledge the suspension in writing, and requires the local commander "who has authority, to convene a Flying Evaluation Board," to "direct an investigation as to why the individual failed to accomplish the medical examination." The commander then should have put a report to higher authorities, or convened a board. But there is no record of either happening.

Bush's commander back in Texas was of course the Lt. Col. Jerry B. Killian who, in between being a personal friend, had written such glowing recommendations of the congressman's son.

All reports suggest that pilots will go a long way to maintain their status. And Maj. Gen. Paul Weaver, who retired as head of the Air National Guard in 2002 put it bluntly, "He should have kept current with his physicals."

A trickle of supportive witnesses now make excuses that since his plane was phasing out, and he was intending to phase himself out, he did not see the need. One of these, retired Air Force Maj. Gen. Donald W. Shepperd, director of the Air National Guard until 1998, said missing a flight physical happens with many part-time pilots. Shepperd said he once did not take an annual flight physical and was grounded. "It's not a big deal," Shepperd said. "You're grounded, and you take it again. As a longtime commander, I saw this happen on a regular basis." [32] But Bush did not take it again.

His office has also explained that he was in Alabama and would have had to go to Houston to take a medical, but those in the know have rubbished this excuse as well. Only a qualified flight surgeon could conduct the medical—and if he had chosen to wander down to Dannelly Air Force Base as he was ordered to, he would have found one available and qualified there.

Bush had everything to gain; the prestige of keeping his wings, the sense of pride and self-worth he obviously derived from being a fighter pilot like his father—and keeping out of trouble with the guard. This is a little like letting off a shotgun next to your ear—failing the medical by nonattendance. Certainly the military tends not be amused by junior ranks deciding what they need or not. His behavior is mysterious—unless you buy the direst stories, that he was covering up for narcotic use.

Following scandals about the extent of narcotic usage in the U.S. military in Vietnam, the Pentagon had introduced mandatory annual drug testing in 1971. Urine samples would be scrutinized for telltale signs of drug use and doctors would even peer up the nostrils of examinees for signs of the damage that snorting cocaine traditionally caused. The 1972 *Air Force Manual* introduced a new form of the old House Un-American Activities Committee's question about communism to deal with the new threat to the realm: "Do you now, or have you ever used or experimented with any drug, other than prescribed by a physician (to include LSD, marijuana, hashish, narcotics, or other dangerous drugs as determined by the attorney general of the United States)?"[33]

Such tests, unless random, would not have caught a Bill Clinton, who famously and fatuously puffed, "but did not inhale," a joint. However, they would have caught someone who took cocaine regularly. There is, of course, no evidence, only persistent rumor, to suggest that this is why the young pilot did not show up for the medical that he was scheduled to have in August 1972 within a month of his birthday.

The long-suffering Dan Bartlett told London's *Sunday Times*, "As he was not flying, there was no reason for him to take the flight exam, and he was not aware of any changes that required a drug test." As excuses go, this is on a par with not inhaling, and also contains other seeds of recrimination. He disobeyed a direct order, rendered "55 weeks" of expensive training useless. And got away with it, which is in its way almost as mysterious as his motivation.

James Moore, the Texas journalist who has been on the case for some time, points out in his book *Bush's War for Reelection*, that the phrase used about the first lieutenant's "failure to accomplish" the medical exam could be more than just military-bureaucratic prose style for not turning up for his medical examination. It could also mean that he did turn

up—and failed some part of the testing. Several guard contemporaries in Washington State were given honorable dis-
charges (of the kind that First Lieutenant Bush eventually
secured) when prohibited substances were found. But this
would require a cover up—of precisely the kind that the con-
fusion in the paper trail suggests may have happened.

In fact, according to the eventually released documents, if
he did turn up at all in Dannelly Air Force Base, he did not
do so until October 28 and 29. There is some doubt about
these documents anyway—and in all logic, if First Lieutenant
Bush had skipped duty all this time because of pressure of his
electoral duties, one does not have to be too cynical to wonder
whether the home stretch to the election—the last two
weeks—would have been the time he picked.

Intrigued by the confused and conflicting excuses put out
by the Bush camp a group of veterans offered a $3,500 reward
for anyone who could verify Bush's Alabama service. Not one
of his six hundred or seven hundred comrades in arms came
forward to share their service memories with a waiting
public. After four years of intensive search, the GOP found
retired Lt. Col. John "Bill" Calhoun, who was the 187th Tactical Recon Group flight safety officer. He conveniently
remembered George Bush showing up for duty at the Dannelly Air Force Base.

The first lieutenant's duty, Calhoun recalled, was to read
safety magazines and flight manuals in an office as he performed his weekend obligations. "I saw him each drill
period," he told AP by telephone from his home in Daytona
Beach, Florida. "He was very aggressive about doing his duty

there. He never complained about it. . . . He was very dedicated to what he was doing in the Guard. He showed up on
time and he left at the end of the day."

It would be great to get a video of Bush "aggressively"
reading the safety manuals and magazines. Could it be that
the puzzled Alfred E. Neuman frown he has whenever he
has to read the teleprompter was somehow mistaken for
aggressiveness and fighting spirit? But then, it raises the
question of why someone who has been trained at the cost
of hundreds of thousands of dollars to fly interceptor planes
should then be allowed to sit in an office reading magazines.

There were other problems, too. Calhoun, a self-confessed
"staunch Republican," also managed to see Bush on duty
with the 187th, variously "at least six," or "eight to ten times"
between May and October—before he applied for duty there
on September 15![34] He says that Bush asked for weekend
drills, but the dates suggested by the White House documents were for weekday duty. Equally, the exoneration that
the White House eventually produced from Bush's records
was a tattered sheet that had no name on it—simply a "W"
and social security number that has been blacked out. It was
cited by Dan Bartlett to prove that it showed credits for two
days at the end of October and two in mid-November. So
that meant that Bush the Younger had only skipped duty in
wartime for a mere six months, so that should be all right
shouldn't it?

On the face of it, Calhoun is unlikely to collect the $3,500
reward from the vets group even if the offer still stands. In
fact, Calhoun may show some of the problems inherent in

alleged false recovered memory cases—and it may be why it
was a disclaimable "Republican close to Bush" rather than the
White House who provided his details to press. If it took
people off the trail then that would be fine, and if the inherent
contradictions in his story did not convince, then there was no
link to the White House.

Jean Sullivan, a Selma Republican leader who worked on
the Blount campaign with Bush also says she saw him in uniform on his way to drills in 1972.[35] One's immediate reaction
was, well, she would say that wouldn't she? A second thought
would be that a lot of people, including later in Harvard, saw
him wearing military gear. It was good for his image.

But despite GOP trawlings, indeed scourings, and regi-
ments of crack reporters scouring the state, they have found
no one else in uniform with more tangible memories of the
first lieutenant's military duties in Alabama. Bearing in
mind the alleged inherent Republican leanings of the military, and the secondhand celebrity status of acquaintance-
ship with a president, this is, frankly, amazing. People will
pay hundreds of thousands of dollars to say they were at a
fund-raising dinner with a president, for a quick hand-
shake and a signed photo. Is it really possible that someone
stood next to the future president at the base and did not
remember?

Indeed, while most newspaper reports stress that there were
hundreds of men in the unit, there is a certain anonymity in a
crowd which almost gives him a let out. More conclusively,
there were only a few dozen pilots, and at least two of them
have an *active* nonrecollection of the president. Bob Mintz and

Paul Bishop are certain they never saw him—because, Mintz told the *Memphis Flyer*, "I was looking for him."

He explained, "I heard someone was coming to drill with us from Texas. And it was implied that it was somebody with political influence. I was a young bachelor then. I was looking for somebody to prowl around with." But Mintz and his colleagues never saw Bush the Younger, despite their active search.[36]

The unit at Dannelly flew F-4s instead of F-102s. Did Bush worry that familiarity with a more modern plane—that was to stay in service until 1996—would enhance his likelihood of actual service? Or did he just not care? In fact, did he worry that if he passed his medical he might have been asked to train on them?

What makes it even more unlikely that his nominal comrades in arms saw yet overlooked him he was how memorable the young Bush was to others. By all accounts, his humor and personality stood out. The blue-rinse set on the Blount campaign remembered him. They called him the Texas Soufflé—all puffed up and full of hot air—for his exaggerated Lone Star behavior as he tried to shed the stigma of being a Yale graduate in the Deep South. Turning up at the crack of noon, he would hoist his cowboy boots onto a campaign office desk and regale the crowd with the previous night's entertainments.

At this stage more Prince Hal than emptily boastful Falstaff, George Bush Jr., as he was known then, reminisced to his colleagues in the campaign about the impunity with which he committed DUI offences back in his Yale days. Blount's nephew, C. Murphy Archibald, said, "He just struck me as a guy who really had an idea of himself as very much a child of privilege, that he wasn't operating by the same rules." Of course, that may be retrospective wisdom, Archibald has been dismissed by other family members as dangerously liberal, but it certainly fits with the pattern of the young Bush's life so far.

There are also allegations that he was fond of coke and marijuana, but no one has come forward to substantiate the stories, so we can discount it in the same way we can discount his National Guard service—since no one has substantiated that either.

Even if he did not dabble in illegal drugs, the young preppie was fond of legal intoxicants and boasted daily at the Blount headquarters about how much he had had to drink the night before. He also had a famous row with his father during his "service" when he took his younger brother Marvin out on a spree and knocked over some garbage cans before they returned to the Bushes' Washington home where the young jock offered his father fisticuffs in the street. This is the one fight we know he definitely volunteered for. Wisely, his father declined.

On the other hand, maybe one of the medical problems he was hiding was a faulty memory, on the lines of his confused and hazy recollections of attendance and duties during this period. The expedient amnesia affects his recollections of drug use as well. He used to refuse to deny or confirm whether he had used illegal drugs. Then he changed his recollections to say that he had not done so since 1974—which implies of course that there is a smoking joint at least out there waiting to bite the commander in chief of the war against drugs in the back-side. But that begs yet another question.

In March 2004, the *Spokane Spokesman-Review* produced yet another angle (March 14, 2004). The F-102 was nuclear capable, and so its pilots came under a national "Human Reliability Program," (HRP) designed to remove pilots whose psychological profile was not up to the strain. No records of First Lieutenant Bush have surfaced that show how he matched the requirements of any such program.

It also pointed out that following the unannounced arrival of a Cuban airliner at a New Orleans airport, in May 1972 the Texas Air National Guard was given enhanced responsibility for guarding U.S. airspace. While the HRP provided yet another possible explanation for Bush's failure to continue flying—the added responsibility for the Texas Air National Guard does raise some questions about the White House's continual assertions that the F-102 and its pilots had in some way become redundant.

As the controversy heated up, as a sort of codicil, the White House discovered the records of Bush's dental exam-ination, signed by Captain J. Andrew Harris dated January 6, 1973. The Montgomery dentist, who was with the 187th at the time, clocked up forty or fifty exams per weekend in the guard, which adds a new dimension for turning up to drill.

But this is one of those alibis that raises more issues than it resolves. Why would Lieutenant Bush have a dental exam-ination in Alabama but for contradictory reasons, or rather excuses, could not make it for a medical by a flight surgeon?

The dentist, Dr. John Andrew Harris, has no specific recollection of the pre-presidential maw, but says it is his signature on the form which showed that the young Bush was
missing his wisdom teeth and tooth number three. "He had
had some cap work." He added to the press, "He was just
another pilot. They had to be seen on an annual basis."

And crucially the date is six months after Bush had missed
his somewhat more important medical examination, and thus
grounded himself as effectively "as letting off a shotgun next
to his ear or going to Canada."

If Lieutenant Bush could make it for dental examination,
then why not the physical? A trickle of supportive witnesses
now make excuses that since his plane was phasing out, and
he was intending to phase himself out, he did not see the need
to maintain his flight status.

But then, there a lot of GIs out in Iraq now, and certainly
there were in Vietnam then, who do not really see the "need"
to maintain their combat status. The decision was not First
Lieutenant's Bush's to make. He himself has claimed that
"there was a conscious decision not to retrain me in an airplane," but has not produced any documentary evidence of
that decision, nor even a person who will admit to having
made such a decision. Dannelly could have offered him a
ground-floor opportunity to check out the F-4 Phantom, the
plane of the future.

Is it gutter politics, as the White House says, to raise such
issues? Far from it. There is little wonder that First Lieutenant Bush's time in Alabama excites such interest, even
before the numerous contradictions and waffly excuses. To

begin with, trained at the taxpayers' considerable expense to fly planes, during a major war, why did he move to Alabama for a non-flying assignment to conduct a political campaign? Why did he not check out those F-4s? Why did he not turn up for the aggressive safety manual reading that was his part in turning back the Red Hordes in Indochina? And why did he not turn up to the crucial medical examination, thus forfeiting the pilot status which had certainly seemed personally important to his self-esteem and was the outcome of a million dollars worth of training: that was, in fact, his duty, his chosen "service" to his country?

The welter of documents that the White House has fluttered out are reminiscent of chaff, the foil dropped by warplanes to frustrate enemy radar. Somewhere in all that chaff is the truth, but former First Lieutenant George W. Bush shows no signs of coming out of the cloud where we can see it, or him in this period. In fact, in his true believer mode, if he were to fess up and repent, bathed in the blood of the lamb, he could redeem himself. But that would require him to grant similar indulgence to others, and contradict the essentially Old Testament vindictiveness he showed in his exercise of one of the few powers of a Texas governor, clemencies on death row.

12 EVASIVE ACTION

IT SEEMS TIMING IS everything. When asked in February 2004 about all these anomalies in Lieutenant Bush's records, White House Press Secretary Scott McClellan accused the journalists responsible of practicing "gutter politics" and "trolling for trash." Asked why what was good for "Slick Willie" as the Bush senior campaign had called Clinton back in 1992, was not good enough for Bush Jr. now, he disingenuously suggested, "I think that you expect the garbage can to be thrown at you in the eleventh hour of a campaign, but not nine months before Election Day."[37]

We have mentioned Clinton before and should really invoke him again. There were many faults in his presidency, not least his pronounced tendency, already visible in his letter to Colonel Holmes, to confuse leadership with going along with the crowd. But while every peccadillo, every suspicion of failings by President Clinton was followed by dogged, intrusive investigations rabid enough to be a witch hunt, George W. Bush's behavior has led to no such inquiries from Congress. Indeed, in 1992 Bush Sr. and Quayle challenged Clinton to release any material about his draft service, with his "draft board, the Selective Service System, the Reserve Officer Training Corps, the army, the navy, the air force, the marines, the coast guard, the United States Departments of State and Justice, any U.S. foreign embassy or consulate."[38]

This was, of course, superfluous since it was almost certainly the Bush crowd that had unearthed and leaked Clinton's letter to Holmes, which pretty much told it all. But Alabama was still a white hole in the records the White House released for Bush's National Guard service.

Bush said, "yeah," when Tim Russert asked him on *Meet the Press* if, like McCain or Wesley Clark, he would be prepared to open up his entire file. But the White House said, "no way" when push came to shove; they are still editing the records. And there are serious doubts about the integrity of the paper trail.

For example, there is no Federal or State investigation into the allegations by former Lt. Col. Bill Burkett of the Texas Air National Guard. He claims that in 1997 he heard his superior officer, Maj. Gen. James II, on the speakerphone with George Bush's Chief of Staff Joe Allbaugh, and Communications Director Dan Bartlett, arranging a laundering of Bush's military records.

He also overheard the conversation the following day, when James had just walked up to the coffee station in the command group offices with two other senior military men, Assistant Adjutant General Wayne Marty and Col. William Goodwin, the chief of staff. He recalls that the State Services Officer Brig. Gen. John Scribner came in with an unidentified man and said "the people from downtown" were coming out to look at the records since Karen Hughes was writing a book on the governor.

Burkett recalls that Marty piped up immediately and added, "and make sure there's nothing there to embarrass the guy." This was overcautious, since Karen Hughes was hardly a muckraking investigator. She was, in fact, Bush's press secretary and she was ghosting what would pass for the president's autobiography, *A Charge to Keep*, which, as one reviewer noted, "will do nothing to dispel" the notion of his lightweightedness, but whose fatuities and evasions have indeed helped this book considerably.

Burkett claims that ten days later, in the former drill hall which by then held the Air National Guard Museum, he saw Scribner at a folding table next to a fifteen-gallon metal waste can. Scribner said he had been told to get the governor's military files together for the book. They jokingly speculated about Bush possibly running for president, but Scribner told them "the files had been gone through over the years. Not as much here as I thought," which could leave the evil-minded to suspect that there had been other, earlier, what one might call antiwinnowers who had thrown out the grain and retained the chaff. However, Burkett soon suspected the reason for that. He saw the contents of the garbage can, and they included both originals and photocopies of pay and performance records—and the name on at least one of them was "Bush, First Lt. George W."

The records the White House released show that as a teenager, Bush had four citations on his driving record for speeding and collisions, which would apparently have required a special enlistment waiver for him to get into the Air National Guard. No such waiver, however, was found in the released documents. It just took three waves of a silver spoon, no doubt, in the Texas office. And a quick flip into the garbage can that Burkett saw may have destroyed the evidence of how the young Bush was absolved and by whom.

Burkett admits he has no smoking gun, but that is the joy of this. Like the dog that did not bark for Sherlock Holmes, George W. Bush's gun never smoked in support of his country, and every effort has been expended to ensure that the fog of deception covers that fact.

Burkett told reporters, "If he's going to be the first president in over one hundred years that puts himself in a uniform and uses the taxpayers' money for a photo opportunity to land on a flight deck and say hooray, he's put it on the table and we deserve to know."

A fellow officer, George Conn, who remembered Burkett telling him about overhearing the phone call, the same night, and who drew his attention to the file sort out in the museum originally verified many elements of Burkett's story. Although he still avers that "Lt. Col. Burkett is an honorable man and does not lie," he has since retracted his memories of the specific conversations and events, a retraction that unkind souls have suggested may be due to his current position as a civilian defense contractor in Germany.

General Daniel James has denied the phone conversation, as did Scribner, Allbaugh, and Bartlett. But as the famous British prostitute, Mandy Rice-Davies, said when prominent politicians denied that they had used her services, "they would, wouldn't they." General James is now head of the Air National Guard across the country, based in Washington. Joe Allbaugh is director of the Federal Emergency Management Agency, appointed by George W. Bush, and Dan Bartlett is White House communications director.

Karen Hughes scrutinized the archives at the Texas Air National Guard, which, if Burkett is to be believed, had already been thoroughly laundered, for *A Charge to Keep*, so we also can assume that every word in the book has been weighed by a committee in the Governor's Mansion in Texas, with a view to electability and plausible deniability if challenged. So it is difficult to keep a straight face when we read, "My time in the guard taught me the importance of a well-trained and well-equipped military. It gave me respect for the chain of command. It showed me, first hand, that given proper training and adequate personnel, the military can accomplish its mission. After all, the military took a novice like me and trained me to be a skilled pilot of high-performance jets. I also learned the lesson of Vietnam. Our nation should slow in engage troops, but when we do so, we must do so with ferocity. We must not go into a conflict unless we go in committed to win. We can never again ask the military to fight a political war. If America's strategic interests are at stake, if diplomacy fails, if no other option will accomplish the objective, the commander in chief must define the mission and allow the military to achieve it."[39]

We talk about the fog of war, but it is nothing to the smog that the Bush team spreads whenever his military posture comes up. From Texas to Alabama, from the war on Iraq to the USS *Lincoln* and the Thanksgiving dinner, they seem chronically incapable of telling the truth about even the smallest details.

There is a children's game in which something is hidden and the other kids shout "warm" or "cold" as the current contestant moves closer to or away from the hiding place. The signals that the administration is sending out are shouting warmer and warmer to the many researchers. By March 2004, the White House referred those who inquired about records to the Pentagon, which in turn refuses to answer any records about the Bush paper trail.

The Air National Guard, now headed by Bush appointee Lt. Gen. Daniel James, who was the Texas Air National Guard adjutant general at the time that Burkett saw the documents, told inquirers that they were under orders not to answer questions. "If it has to do with George W. Bush, the Texas Air National Guard, or the Vietnam War, I can't talk with you," said Charles Gross, chief historian for the National Guard Bureau in Washington, D.C to Bill Morlin and Karen Dorn Steele of the *Spokane Spokesman-Review*. They also report Rose Bird, Freedom of Information Act officer for the bureau, saying that her office stopped taking records requests on Bush's military service in mid-February and is directing all inquiries to the Pentagon.

In the meantime, while the White House felt that George W. Bush's medical records deserved privacy, the Texas National Guard showcased the state surgeon general who shared Bill Burkett's medical records with the press in an attempt to discredit his testimony. It could just be a coincidence that his the medical disability rating was dropped from 50 percent to 30 percent. But anyone who thinks that probably believes in the tooth fairy.

After corroborating his story for so long, his old friend George Conn's change of heart, coupled with his endorsement of Burkett's integrity should have led the media to wonder why, what sort of pressure led to his semi-retraction. Instead, many of them presented it as an absolution of Bush. It is, of course, no such thing. While the administration has suggested that Burkett has an ulterior motive in his quarrel with the guard for better recognition of the illness picked up in Panama, in fact every one of their witnesses has a lot to lose if they did not deny the story.

Typical of how much of the media have played the Bush military record, they have weighed each item of news with a presumption of presidential innocence that the facts tend not to support. Whether or not those records were taken out and trashed in the Texas Air National Guard Museum, there are many crucial records missing, and many unexplained questions about Bush's service, and a pattern of stalling from the administration and bureaucracy when the chaff it released earlier did not divert all incoming inquiries. Occam's razor indicates that Burkett's answer fits the observable pattern.

13 THE HARVARD YEARS

BUSH AND PULL

THE PERVASIVE NETWORK OF nepotism in Texas worked for the guard—but it is a testament to the academic integrity of the University of Texas Law School that even while his father was a congressman, they would not admit the young lieutenant with the unimpressive transcripts from Yale. It took the mysterious workings of the other Old Money network at Harvard to get him admitted to the Business School—that old white magic, affirmative action Ivy League style, worked for him. It is clear from his subsequent business career, that this was the right choice by all parties.

At Harvard, Bartlett says Bush was transferred to a reserve unit in Boston for the rest of his time. But no one else seems to have noticed it. He did not abandon his uniform. No, sir. A classmate recalls him sitting at the back of the class wearing a National Guard bomber jacket, chewing tobacco and spitting the noxious residue into a cup. But he did not do that all the time. There is the famous picture of him, unkempt with a big gum bubble coming out his mouth. There is perhaps some comfort to be taken that he does not seem to have tried to chew gum and tobacco at the same time.

There are profound difficulties in reconciling the official records of the last year and a half of Bush's term in the National Guard before he went to Harvard with anything resembling reality. Someone entered him for several days in Alabama that no one there remembers him doing. The form this took was "points" entered for days of drill that would qualify for the minimum service requirement. To be fair, we should add that during his flight training and service at Ellington in previous years, he had amassed far more than the annual minimum, but there was no provision to roll those over to the very lean and fallow years that followed in 1972 and 1973.

We know he was in Washington over Christmas, because that was when and where he offered his father a fistfight over his drunken driving escapade with his younger brother. His official story has him returning to Houston after Christmas to start work at project PULL. And then, mysteriously he turned up for his first and only recorded and attested day of duty between April 1972 and May 1973—a dental examination in the Alabama base where no one had seen him at any other time, and which he was supposed to have quit to return to duty at Ellington AFB, Texas.

Bush features his time at the PULL project in his autohagiography, in which he says John White, a Houston Oiler tight end, asked him to come to work there. It is not being overly churlish to raise an eyebrow at the likelihood of the young George W. Bush suddenly spontaneously discovering deep charitable impulses that would lead him to drop his life of carousing and sending coded racist electoral messages for Republican friends of the family in order to move to active participation in a minority-targeted poverty program. As we have noted elsewhere, any sense of *noblesse oblige* was left behind in the East Coast family home's attics when the Bushes transplanted to the tougher climes of Texas.

A more refined suggestion for his work at PULL is that after the near punch-up, his exasperated father told him to shape up and mandated the job as a condition of continuing parental support. This version would have him dragging young Bush along, metaphorically at least, by the ear. However, that raises the question—he had a "job" he could go to serving as jet pilot in the Texas Air National Guard, so why didn't he go there? Why in fact did he stay away, effectively AWOL, from the Air National Guard during this period?

On May 2, we know that no one in the Texas ANG had seen him, because his officer evaluation was returned with the comment from Lt. Col. William Harris that "Lt. Bush has not been observed at this unit during the period of report. A civilian occupation made it necessary for him to move to Montgomery, Alabama. He cleared this base May 15, 1972 and has been performing equivalent training in a non-flying status with the 187 Tac Recon Gp. Dannelly ANG Alabama."

Even his biggest fan Killian could cover up for him no more and "concurs" with Harris' comments. The air force, being bureaucratic and non-Texan did not think this was sufficient, and requested form 77A "so that officer can be rated in the position he held." It adds snippily, "This officer should have been reassigned in May 1972 if he is no longer training in his AFSC or with his unit of assignment."

Texas waited until First Lieutenant Bush was safely discharged and in Harvard to send in the form saying that he was "not rated for the period 1 May 1972 through 30 Apr 73. Report for this period not available for administrative reasons." We can presume that "administrative reasons" covers a multitude of sins of both omission and commission.

Somehow, immediately following that May 2 report, the lieutenant springs to life and is marked down as performing thirty-six days of duty. That is almost full time—and even more intriguing because his memoirs claim he was working with Project PULL "full-time." He said he worked there for nine months, and was in Harvard by the Fall. So he put in almost eight working weeks with the National Guard, while holding down a full time position at PULL. In addition, Harvard had accepted him earlier in the year, so whatever he did now, he had an exit strategy. Did he begin by thinking that since no one had noticed his absence, and he had friends in the Texas ANG, he could sort of just drift off to Harvard with no one noticing.

So the most likely hypothesis is that following that May 2 report, dictated by the bureaucratic timetable, the officers in the ANG realized that it was their careers on the line, not just this spoiled preppy. They took action to ensure that Lt. Bush had sufficient points for an honorable discharge. Maybe, knowing that he had been accepted for Harvard, the usual Texas fixers got together and conspired to have entered up for all those days of drill since they were the minimum necessary for an honorable discharge.

Otherwise, no one knows what he did with the National Guard. Why did he not attend his flight medical examination? Why was there no examining board to find out why he had "failed to accomplish his medical examination" the year before? It has been suggested that he was allowed to book those days at PULL as drill. It does look entirely plausible that he was marked attending when he didn't, since neither he nor anybody else has suggested what he actually did for those days.

While we cannot say definitively what the problem is here, there is indeed a smell of rotten fish emanating. One solution was that of James H. Hatfield, whose book *Fortunate Son*, was pulled from the shelves by St. Martin's Press within one week of publication in 1999 after the Bush family and the Republicans launched a huge campaign against it and its author, who they revealed had had a murder conviction many years before.

Hatfield quoted "a high-ranking advisor to Bush" who confirmed to him that Bush was arrested for cocaine possession in Houston in 1972, and had the record expunged by a judge who was "a fellow Republican and elected official" who helped Bush get off "with a little community service at a minority youth center instead of having to pick cotton on a Texas prison farm."

Hatfield also quoted a former Yale classmate who told him: "George W. was arrested for possession of cocaine in 1972, but due to his father's connections, the entire record was expunged by a state judge whom the older Bush helped get elected. It was one of those 'behind closed doors in the judge's chambers' kind of thing between the old man and one of his Texas cronies who owed him a favor. . . . There's only a handful of us that know the truth."

He quoted another "longtime Bush friend" who used an appropriate analogy bearing in mind the young Bush's scholastic record, "Say you get a D in algebra . . . and now you're going to be required to repeat the class the following year, but your teacher says if you promise to be tutored during the summer by a friend of hers who's good in math, she'll change the D to a C. You spend a few hours a week during the summer vacation learning all about arithmetical operations and relationships, and then the teacher issues you a new report card, replacing the old one on file in the principal's office. . . . Something akin to that scenario is what happened with Bush in 1972."

Hatfield also alleges that when he asked Scott McClellan to comment on the allegation of a former Yale classmate of Bush's that the presidential hopeful was arrested for cocaine possession in 1972 and had his record expunged in exchange for community service at Project PULL, McClellan muttered, "Oh, shit," followed by, "No comment."

As they say, "Houston, we have a problem." On July 20, 2001, Hatfield was found dead with a suicide note in an Arkansas motel room. This was after he had found another publisher and the book was selling well. At the very least, if this had been Clinton whose trail he had been following, we would have had a special prosecutor on the case. One of the sources he later claimed was Karl Rove, who is hardly likely to corroborate the tale.

But before rushing off to dismiss it entirely, and even while making a presumption of innocence until proven guilty, there are some strange circumstances surrounding the case. The Bush campaign has never outright denied cocaine use. They simply said that he had not used any illegal drugs since 1974, which in less-privileged mortals would be an implicit confession that he had indeed indulged before then.

Bush declined to comment directly on the cocaine allegations, saying only that he had made mistakes in his youth but had not used illegal drugs since at least 1974. No witnesses came forward to support the allegations. George Bush the Elder denied the allegations that his son was arrested for cocaine possession in 1972 and that a Texas state judge wiped the arrest off the younger Bush's record. But then, as a sort of pre-Valentine's Day present, on February 13, 2004, Helen Thomas, the veteran White House correspondent reduced the same Scott McClellan to incoherent evasion when, without mentioning Hatfield, she asked McClellan if the president had been ordered to do community service. McClellan wriggled, squirmed, tried counter-attacking, and was being so obviously evasive that the rest of the press corps joined in trying to get him to either say yes or no or that he would approach the president to answer the question. The full, barely controlled panicked response is in the appendix, and should perhaps be set next to the refusal to deny categorically the use of illegal drugs before 1974.

One does not have to be too partisan to smell a fish here. We do not know its size, or its species, or even where it is lurking, but you do not need the nose of a conspiracy theorist to smell it. It is clear that the Bush campaign thinks, indeed knows, that somewhere out there is some tangible piece of evidence, or credible witness, who can give the lie to any absolute denial. There is simply no other reason for such obfuscation or refusal to answer the question.

Indeed one of the more plausible suggestions would explain why Burkett thought he saw the pay records being trashed. The officers may have entered him up on the forms necessary for his discharge but balked at putting him on pay for those days, since that would have been serious financial fraud, beyond the call of nepotism.

The destruction of the pay records would remove the discrepancy, and cover not just First Lieutenant George W. Bush, but all the other local Texan officers who had put their butts on the line for the brat.

In the end, he exited the Texas Air National Guard almost as expeditiously as he had entered, and almost certainly with the same patronage-boost afterburning his exit as his entrance. In September 5, 1973, although he had at least eight months to run, he applied for an early discharge to go to Harvard Business School and a nominal sinecurist reserve appointment to a base in Massachusetts where he did not even have to pretend to attend drill, or aggressively attack those safety manuals. His honorable discharge was approved in a day—he surely knew it would. He may have been going to Cambridge—but the Texas Air National Guard had to stay behind where the Bushes could come after them. And that ubiquitous signature recommending approval of his request was of none other than his old friend

Lt. Col. Jerry Killian. Bush's letter had mentioned how much he had enjoyed his time with the unit. "You bet," as they say in some parts of the South.

Much has been made of that "honorable discharge," but honor is a very elastic concept in the South, one that has traditionally included opening a door for a lady and bringing the matches to a lynch party. In the Air National Guard, the reasons for an honorable discharge can add up to, "Glad to see the back of you." They include drug abuse, failure to participate, the inability of the service to locate the discharge, and not meeting the requirements for medical examination. They may not have broken young George's sword and ripped off his epaulettes, but they were hardly pinning a medal on him.

Perhaps the kindest suggestion is that First Lieutenant George W. Bush was simply such a liability that they were glad to get rid of him, fifty-five weeks of expensive pilot training and all. And imagine poor Lt. Col. Killian, who had helped engineer fast-track entry into the guard, supersonic speed promotion, and written such glowing reports, only to find that his blue-eyed boy was effectively AWOL, and had certainly lost interest in flying—on air force planes anyway.

He may have been burying his own mistakes, as well as the trail of patronage by getting the spoilt Ivy League brat back up to the Northeast. But you can't keep even an overcompensating adoptive Texan away from the Lone Star State for too long. He was soon back, and his business career, parlaying other people's money and influence to disguise his lack of personal success was everything that a close examination of his military career would leave you to expect.

In 1978, Bush the Younger became involved in politics in his own right and ran for a congressional district that stretched from Lubbock to his hometown of Midland. Kent Hance was a Democratic state senator, schooled in the skull-duggery of Texas politics and when Bush tried his sopho-moric beer-keg canvassing with an ad in the Texas Tech student paper, the *University Daily*, offering free beer at a Bush rally, he discovered that Davenport Armour Council was not the same as Southern Bible Belt politics.

In the self-deprecatory style that makes him almost likeable if he were not acting the fool a little too well, Bush told Yale graduates when he went back there, "If you're like me, you won't remember everything you did here." He reminisced about enrolling in a Japanese haiku course, for which an adviser "said I should focus on English. I still hear that quite often. But my critics don't realize I don't make verbal gaffes. I'm speaking in the perfect forms and rhythms of ancient haiku." He also implicated Yale in his famously fractured syntax. "I want the entire world to know this—everything I know about the spoken word, I learned right here at Yale."

But Yale it seems was poor preparation for down-and-dirty Texas politics. There is a venerable tradition in Amer-ican politics that candidates float to victory on a sea of booze. Bush's namesake George Washington complained of the cost of being elected to the Virginian House of Burgesses in 1758, which included forty gallons of rum punch, twenty-eight gallons of wine, forty-three gallons of beer, and twenty-six gallons of Barbados's best rum. However, George W. was, as Lloyd Bentsen might have said, no George Washington, and the Great Awakening had turned things around. There are even nineteenth-century Currier and Ives prints of Washington, where, after the temperance movement had taken a grip, glasses and punch bowls were bowdlerized out of the founding father's grip.

Hance's campaign sent out a letter addressed to "Dear Fellow Christians," which appealed to both good ol' Southern religion and populism, informing them that "Mr. Bush has used some of his vast sums of money . . . to persuade young college students to vote for and support him by offering free alcohol to them." In contrast to Hance's self-evident virtues, not least of which was being a born Texan and not an implied Ivy League carpetbagger, the letter used the beer bash to prove that Bush's tactics did "not indicate the same high character."[40]

Bush himself later reminisced, during the '94 governor's race that the letter was his "first confrontation with cheap-shot politics." It was not so cheap, since, of course, if he had been attuned to local folkways, he would have realized the effect of a free-beer offer on local Baptists. And, of course, this was not the first time he had come across cheap political shots. He and Allison and Rove and others had specialized in dishing them out to others, but it is always amusing to see a bully cry when he is whacked back. The self-righteous indignation at others hitting back that we see here has been a constant of Bush campaigns ever since.

Back then young George was not totally in touch with his inner temperance soul, so he offered his butt to the Hance campaign, which happily took advantage of it. He bleated that it was not "fair" and, of course, registered the tactic for his own future use, not least appealing to fundamentalist sentiment.

Kent Hance, who trounced Bush's congressional hopes, insinuated that Bush was not a true Texan and accused him of "riding his daddy's coattails," and made much of Bush going to Yale and Harvard, comparing these disadvantages with his own attendance at University of Texas Law School. "In the panhandle, if it's Texas Tech versus Yale, Tech will beat Yale every time. That's not even a close game," Hance told the *Texas Observer*, with the air of stating self-evident truths.

In fact, there is more truth evident below the surface, in the light of Bush's failure to make the grade for the Texas School of Law, and his legacied entrance to Harvard. Similarly, the young candidate discovered that it took more than a few phone calls to ex–Skull and Bonesmen and friends of his father to win an election. It took *lots* of phone calls, first to raise the money, then to hire the down and dirty political talent to erase that silver spoon from his image.

In fact, he raised $400,000, largely from old family friends and fellow Bonesmen, which Hance was also able to play cleverly as out-of-state money coming to corrupt the pure stream of the Lone Star State's elections. But how little political difference there was between them was shown when Hance defected to the GOP in 1985, sent $10,000 to junior Bush's campaign for governor, and became enlisted as a "pioneer" in his presidential campaign.

They are a forgiving lot in Texas. As long as you are rich, white, well-connected, and not on death row. Family, friends, and faith. Semper Fi!

14 BAYONETS AND BALLOTS

BUT WHILE BUSH'S DESIRE to emulate his dad, let alone strut like a Texan, explains a lot of his military posturing and evasiveness about his lack of actual military experience, it would be dangerous to underestimate the political calculations here. Karl Rove and company. obviously calculate that all these recent visits to bases have a political dividend. Not even a giant cuttlefish would use so much ink to cover the nugatory military career of Bush the Younger, unless they thought that it had tangible political benefits.

So the presumed rationale for someone like Bush joining the guard was to preserve his military credentials while dodging the one in three odds of actually being drafted, although, of course, many of those who were not drafted also invoked bad knees, bad backs, or whatever other ailment that could be mimicked effectively in the days before ubiquitous MRIs.

Not surprisingly, almost the whole of Bush's entourage found themselves too preoccupied to go to war—and one can wager that few of their offspring are in Iraq now, unless they are working for Halliburton. So, in abstract, if a majority of that generation avoided, evaded, or otherwise missed duty in Vietnam, we can presume that, if anything, their sympathies lie with the Clintons, Deans, and others who managed to avoid risking their lives for a war they did not believe in.

In any case, medal-bedecked veteran or passport-stamped draft dodger, what that generation may tend to forget is that for most younger Americans, which includes almost everyone under fifty who has not had the threat of the draft looming over them, the Vietnam War is almost as far back in history as the First World War was for the Vietnam generation. The draft in WWI was not a hot-button issue for the sixties generation, so those who have succeeded the baby boomers may be a bit perplexed by the fuss.

If that is so, it is not really too surprising that polls showed that the renewed controversy over Bush's murky military résumé did not have a huge effect on overall voting. According to Gallup in February 2004, as the press corps tried to make sense from the spotty acronym-strewn National Guard records the White House had passed on, 56 percent of the people polled said that Bush did "nothing seriously wrong," while 33 percent considered that had done "something unethical" and 8 percent said he had done "something illegal." Indeed, 42 percent say he "did his duty for the country during the Vietnam War," while 40 percent disagreed.[41]

Those Gallup figures derive from a range of attitudes.

After all, many Bush contemporaries were pulling strokes to evade service. Out of just under 19 million men whose age put them in consideration for the draft between 1964 and 1973, only some 9 million actually served on active duty, including 1.7 million draftees, while another 2 million joined Bush in the Reserves or the National Guard. In 1966, there were more fathers of draft age, deferred from service than the total 2.6 million men and women who served in the entire conflict.[42] One of those was Vice President Dick Cheney, now a hawkish power center in his position as the most hyperactive and influential vice president on record.

The most obvious real-time experiment on the importance of military service has to be the election for two terms of Bill Clinton, vilified so frequently as a draft dodger. The vilification shows that some people care: but more vote the other way. One could even suspect that many of them had fixed opinions about the Democrats, Clinton and his generation, so the draft was just an issue to hit an already loathed politician. In that case, we could perhaps assume that, in the end, the kind of people who had expressed the most concern about Clinton's military career would not really worry about Bush's. Clinton was an intellectual, with a dyke-feminist spouse and fond of colored folks, so his draft record was really just apt commentary. In contrast, they like Bush anyway: he's Texan, Christian, against taxes, and likes NASCAR and wearing uniforms, so let's cut him some slack.

In the present partisan state of American politics, the number of declared Republicans who will find the faintest speck of clay on the feet of their candidate is strictly limited.

In this they have been helped by the general deferential demeanor of the American press, who have not really asked the serious question lest it tend toward lèse-majesté, or worse, since that sounds French, disloyalty. That question is, of course, "If you keep talking about patriotism and sacrifice, why didn't you go the extra nine yards to ensure that you did your bit in Vietnam when your government and party was telling you that you were needed?"

But both parties have tended to take their hard-core voters for granted and aim at the middle of the road. For the last election Bush projected, and indeed invented an entirely spurious compassionate conservatism to attract them. This time it is Bush, Warlord and Protector in Times of Terror, which may account for the fevered reaction of the campaign to digs about Bush the Younger's military career. If the issue is taxes, you do not need a warrior in the White House. But if the issue is security, you may prefer that.

Madison's warning about the dangers of manipulated external threats was dangerously prescient: the Bush campaign is based on the manipulation of a real or imagined external threat which of itself conjures up support for an ominous and dangerous militarization of society. Certainly, the war on terror is deliciously vague. In many ways, it is even better than the war against communism. Communists tended to identify themselves openly, but terror by its nature is clandestine, so you can find it anywhere you want to identify it.

Naturally, Bush the Younger plays up the threat, which after the smoldering charnel house of the World Trade Center is not that difficult, and then present himself as the answer, wrapped in the flag and a uniform. It helps, of course, that it is a task that clearly gives him a lot of job satisfaction, but it also makes him vulnerable and nervous since as Richard Cohen pointed out in the *Washington Post* (February 10, 2004):

> The reason is that this time he is likely to compete against a genuine war hero. John Kerry did not duck the war. But George Bush did. He did so by joining the National Guard. Bush now wants to drape the Vietnam-era guard with the bloodied flag of today's Iraq-serving guard—'I wouldn't denigrate service to the guard,' Bush warned during his interview with Russert—but the fact remained that back then the guard was where you went if you did not want to fight. That was the case with me. I opposed the war in Vietnam and had no desire to fight it. Bush, on the other hand, says he supported the war—as long, it seems, as someone else fought it. When Bush attempts to drape the flag of today's guard over the one he was in so long ago, when he warns his critics to remember that 'there are a lot of really fine people who have served in the National Guard and who are serving in the National Guard today in Iraq,' then he is doing now what he was doing then: hiding behind the ones who were really doing the fighting. It's about time he grew up.

So how does it play with military themselves? Better than

it should, but perhaps less than the GOP hoped. In any case, a surprising proportion of the armed forces vote, certainly in comparison with the traditionally low turnout of actual civilians.

A total of 74 percent of all members of the uniformed services cast ballots in November 2000—72 percent overseas, 76 percent stateside. Overall, only 51 percent of all eligible Americans voted. In all, 258,000 active-duty military, 118,000 family members and about 87,000 Department of Defense civilian employees stationed overseas during the 2000 federal-election cycle voted.

There are also the 27 million veterans whom Bush keeps invoking. With their families, that's almost a quarter of all voters. For many of these, their military service may be an episode of minimal importance in their lives. However probably, similar if not higher numbers of self-nominated veterans vote conscientiously. Even though the American Legion and Veterans of Foreign Wars only amass 4.9 million members out of 27 million veterans, this self-selecting group is assumed to speak for the whole, but since their leaderships are conservative in their politics that probably exaggerates any rightward-leaning by actual veterans.

In November 2000, with thousands of military personnel based in Florida, the absentee ballots from the military were a crucial factor in the messy result in that election. The GOP's infamous Florida Secretary of State Katherine Harris, the co-chairwoman of Bush's Florida campaign, advised county election boards that state law required the overseas ballots to have a postmark.

When they saw the narrowness of the gap between Gore

and Bush in 2000, the GOP launched an assault on alleged
Democratic foot-dragging over counting absentee military
ballots and Rep. Steve Buyer, an Indiana Republican, abused
his chairmanship of a House Armed Services Subcommittee
to get the phone numbers and e-mail addresses of servicemen
who had cast votes for the Florida Republican Party.[43]

The issue dragged on for months, but no one ever tested
the assumption that these votes were all for the GOP. In
fact, insofar as they represented the votes of black Floridian
members of the armed forces, they were almost certainly
cast for Gore.

The GOP claims that Bob Dole got 54 percent of the military absentee votes in the 1996 presidential election compared
with his 43 percent overall. And although he was a genuine,
wounded, war veteran, they expected unwounded unwarred
Bush to do better.

While the Republicans assume they have a lock on military
votes, it seems that it may not be true in practice. For a start,
many of the enlisted men and women come from minorities
and backgrounds where they traditionally vote Democratic,
and retain those habits afterward. Among officers, the
Republican vote is probably higher—but the equivalent social
milieu would be in civilian life as well.

However, it is not all so clear-cut. Sociologist Charles
Moskos surveyed the military in Kosovo and found that
while the officers did indeed tend to vote Republican,
enlisted men and women divide their votes between the two
parties. Among the 320 U.S. soldiers in Kosovo in September
2000, 32 percent described themselves as liberal, 44 percent

as middle-of-the-road, and only 24 percent as conservative. Since enlisted personnel outnumber officers six to one and about 37 percent of the active-duty force is nonwhite, the pressure of outside reality is clearly impinging on the military.

It has been argued that as the best integrated body in American life, one of the few, if not the only institution where white people customarily take orders from blacks, such ethnic differences may not carry over into the military. On one level, we can adduce Colin Powell's membership of the Republican cabinet as evidence for that.

On the other hand, Powell himself does not always exude ecstasy at the company he is forced to keep, and it would take an extremely masochistic black Floridian to vote Republican in a state where the party was visibly using almost everything short of an outright color bar to ensure a low black turnout. Indeed, with such a high minority representation in the army and the high turnout of the military voters compared with civilians, it could be suggested that this would lead to a higher vote by Democratic supporters who, in civilian life, may not have voted.

However, sometimes, as the White House projection of the president's military career shows, perceptions are important and can shape reality even if, and indeed especially when, they are out of touch with it. Certainly in Florida, and a lot of these states with big bases in key states that Bush hoped and needed to win, the GOP staff assumed that the absentee military ballots would be coming to them.

In contrast, a poll conducted in September 2003, six months after Bush had declared victory in Iraq among military relatives showed the president's approval rate at 36 percent, far lower than in the general electorate. Military Families Speak Out founder, Nancy Lessin, stepmother of a marine, suggested why: "Soldiers are being used as cannon fodder."[44] And it seems they know it.

It seems likely that there is indeed a swing vote out there, a crucial one in crucial states, where the issue of George W. Bush and his military record is an important issue. Karl Rove is no sentimentalist, and the frenzy with which the White House has fought back accusations on Bush in Alabama should suggest, in the words of that great military strategist, Mao Tse-tung, "To be attacked by the enemy is not a bad thing but a good thing."

In any case, the warlord persona is certainly designed to go beyond the armed forces. The projection of George W. Bush, as the commander in chief is a response to the paranoia about the terrorist threat, played up at every opportunity. At this stage, it is aimed at all those people who still jump every time Tom Ridge cries "Wolf!" yet again.

But as readers have may now have begun to suspect, the commander in chief is about as authentic as the Wizard of Oz as a veteran and a military commander.

15 COMMANDER IN CHIEF

WHILE WE JUDGE A commander by his battles, we weigh a commander in chief by his wars. Any president would have to go into Afghanistan to break Osama bin Laden's territorial redoubts. And, at first, the rapid collapse of the Taliban seemed to vindicate the war presidency of George W. Bush.

But how would history regard Roosevelt and Churchill if two years after the invasion of Germany, Allied troops still did not control most of the country and were still under fire trying to find Hitler in Bavaria, while they had sent the bulk of the Allied Forces to invade and occupy Argentina because Churchill was convinced that it was Peron who was really behind the Blitz?

Bush's self-delusion became apparent after September 11. Goaded by his neocon advisers, he had Iraq in his sights from the beginning. Bush's megalomania, even in Bob Woodward's friendly account, should have caused much more concern.

GREAT COMMANDERS

So Bush's military virtue, rather than following in his father's contrail, rather recalls one quasi-historical figure, the Duke of Plaza-Toro, from Gilbert and Sullivan's *Gondoliers*.

In enterprise of martial kind,
When there was any fighting,
He led his regiment from behind—
He found it less exciting.
But when away his regiment ran,
His place was at the fore, O—
That celebrated,
Cultivated,
Underrated
Nobleman,
The Duke of Plaza-Toro!

ALL.
In the first and foremost flight, ha, ha!
You always found that knight, ha, ha!
That celebrated,
Cultivated,
Underrated
Nobleman,
The Duke of Plaza-Toro!

DUKE.
When, to evade Destruction's hand,
To hide they all proceeded,
No soldier in that gallant band
Hid half as well as he did.
He lay concealed throughout the war,
And so preserved his gore, O!
That unaffected,
Undetected,
Well-connected

Bush told Rove, "Just like my father's generation was called in World War II, now our generation is being called . . ." "I'm here for a reason," he said, "and this is going to be how we're going to be judged."

Woodward referred to "Bush's belief that he must state new strategic direction or policy with bold, clear moves. And because it would be the policy of the United States, the only superpower, the rest of the world would have to move over. . . ."[45]

This messianic approach is very disturbing. It sounds more like a megalomanic Mahdi rather than an elected president, one of whose titular functions is commander in chief of the armed forces. After all, Queen

Elizabeth II is also officially commander in chief of the British forces, but no one has been daft enough to let her or her ancestors interfere in military affairs for several centuries now.

In any case, while there may well have been sound reasons for the president not to fly to Washington on September 11, and even for Cheney to stay away from the White House in case it was a target, "to ensure continuity of government," to equate himself and his draft-evading cronies with the Second World War generation, is beyond pomposity. It is a betrayal of the current generation whose lives he is putting at risk not just in the dubious battle that is a soldier's lot, but in a dubious war.

Warrior,
The Duke of Plaza-Toro!

ALL.
In every doughty deed, ha, ha!
He always took the lead, ha, ha!
That unaffected,
Undetected,
Well-connected
Warrior,
The Duke of Plaza-Toro!

DUKE.
When told that they would all be shot
Unless they left the service,
That hero hesitated not,
So marvellous his nerve is.
He sent his resignation in,
The first of all his corps, O!
That very knowing,
Overflowing,
Easy-going
Paladin,
The Duke of Plaza-Toro!

ALL.
To men of grosser clay, ha, ha!
He always showed the way, ha, ha!
That very knowing,
Overflowing,
Easy-going
Paladin,
The Duke of Plaza-Toro!
That very knowing,
Overflowing,
Easy-going
Paladin,
The Duke of Plaza-Toro! Plaza-Toro!

Since Bush the Younger, as we have seen, is deeply attached to the title of commander in chief, he can hardly complain if we judge him by that standard. The reputation of a great commander is not made by battles alone, but by his conduct of wars. Was the war on Iraq necessary? Was it against the right enemy? Were appropriate allies mustered to help? Did it leave the country absolutely and relatively stronger afterwards than before? When it was fought, was it on the right battlefields? Had all steps been taken to ensure against failure? Were the troops properly fed and equipped? Were deaths minimized, the wounded assured quick medical treatment? And were the survivors and disabled looked after?

On all these criteria, Commander in Chief Bush has blown it. The revelations of Paul O'Neill, Richard A. Clarke, and even now Bob Woodward, show the White House has been exorcising its own obsessions rather than punishing al-Qaeda, let alone preventing it from attacking again.

All of these witnesses testify that even before September 11, George W. Bush and his advisors were obsessed with Iraq and Saddam Hussein to an unhealthy and irrational degree and that even after the attacks on the World Trade Center, despite a complete lack of evidence, George W. Bush was convinced that Saddam Hussein was behind them.

The president let those obsessions transform worldwide support for the United States and its actions in Afghanistan after September 11 into almost global revulsion for himself and his policy in less than a year. In its place all he could assemble was a "Potemkin coalition," a desperate attempt to shore up the international legitimacy of the attack on Iraq by drafting some weak and a few willing leaders—willing, that is, to defy their own publics.

We can sense some of the embarrassment involved when Colin Powell announced that there were thirty countries in the "coalition of the willing" and "fifteen other nations, for one reason or another, who do not wish to be publicly named, but will be supporting the coalition." Just what you need behind you in time of war—fifteen shrinking allies who are so convinced of your cause that they want to hide their faces!

In fact, the anonymity of the fifteen was less to do with any concern on their part than with Washington's embarrassment about them. After all, bullies are sometimes embarrassed by the fawning adulation of the weak.

The transformation from having the support of the world to being the deranged global ogre took about a year. The United States backed a motley and not necessarily deeply moral Northern Alliance in Afghanistan, which most people saw as part of the problem there as much as they were part of any solution. The heavily armed warlords had been the losers in the meltdown of Afghanistan and were every bit as murderous as the Taliban—just more corruptible and less theological in their mayhem.

In the name of the "war on terror," Bush and his administration embraced some of the most vicious and tyrannical regimes in Asia. Uzbekistan, a country which has all the political practices of the Beria era from the fifties, which is when its ex-Communist president learned his tricks, but has none of the social safety net that the old Soviets offered, was suddenly our frontline ally. Bush and company enlisted Pakistan, whose secret service and army had been backing the Taliban and to a large extent Osama bin Laden.

Bush and company's decisions in Afghanistan reflected their phobias. U.S. troops must not be involved in "nation-building," since this was a namby-pamby multilateral thing reminiscent of Clinton. U.S. troops were there to fight wars, and let lesser breeds do the cleaning up afterward.

The hasty exit from Afghanistan, leaving the Northern Alliance and the Taliban still at large has left the country two years later, with only small units of special forces still involved in trying to ferret out Osama bin Laden who has, of course, not been found. Instead, hundreds of thousands of troops are bogged down in a war in Iraq, where they have found Saddam Hussein, but where the war is going on regardless and relentless.

16 WHY IRAQ?

IN THE OLD DAYS scientists used to look for the "missing link," the fossils that bridged the gap between stupid monkeys and clever men. There is a similar missing link between the George W. Bush and a coherent foreign policy.

Saddam Hussein was an evil dictator. He had, as Bush the Younger told the United Nations one year after September 11, used poison gas on his own people. He had made war on his neighbors, beginning with Iran. He was *not* cooperating with the UN weapons inspectors. On the other hand, as the listening delegates knew well, it was Bush Sr. and Ronald Reagan who had encouraged his war on Iran, had helped cover him diplomatically at the time he was gassing Iraqis and Iranians, and had provided the sinews of war, the credits, and the weaponry to accomplish all of the above.

One of more risible elements of the Bush administration's much touted "axis of evil" hypothesis was that, as a metaphor, it was a total failure. Far from being on an axis, the rulers of Iran and Iraq hated each other—almost as much as they both hated al-Qaeda and Osama bin Laden. In fact, the only thing they had in common was they were both hated by Israel, which had not stopped the Iranians doing some weapons trading with the Israelis under Reagan administration aegis as part of Contragate, nor Iraq trying to cut a deal with Israel to get the Americans off their backs under Clinton.

So the Iranian delegation was not sure whether to be pleased or surprised at their promotion from charter member of the axis of evil to first victim of iraqi aggression in Bush's UN speech, but they kept their cool. It was just as well. Apart from this aberration, and despite their cooperation against the Taliban, they soon discovered that the axis was their rightful home, second on the shit list for George Bush, Ariel Sharon, and the neocons. Saddam Hussein, of course, remained at the top of the list.

The delegates were puzzled, and it showed. Most of what Bush told them was true, although no one was buying his line that Iraq and al-Qaeda were in cahoots, and some were not entirely sure that Iraq had indeed tried to assassinate Bush Sr. back in 1993. They also knew that most of the sins that he was laying at Saddam Hussein's door were perpetrated when the Iraqi dictator was the West's great white hope against Iranian fundamentalism. They were even gratified that a president whose cabinet members were often publicly scornful of the UN should come to them for help. The one tangible point he made was Saddam Hussein's exclusion of UN weapons

inspectors. But what did this have to do with September 11,
or Osama bin Laden?

More to the point, almost everyone concerned in foreign
affairs, internationally and domestically, was convinced of one
thing: if Iraq had any weapons, they were no threat to the United
States. Bush's claim to the United Nations that there was a connection between the attack on the World Trade Center and Iraq
was, and is, clearly preposterous. The Ba'athist Party was a secularist, fascist party, which tolerated Islam as long as it controlled the mosques tightly. Al-Qaeda and Saddam Hussein
were as likely to team up together as the pope and Oral Roberts
were to have a tag-preaching team.

It would have been more reassuringly rational if the White
House were just after Iraqi oil, as many conspiracy theorists
have posited. In fact, in the long run, the precarious Arab
regimes that sit on much of the region's oil may not survive
the popular backlash from the unilateral war and protracted
occupation of Iraq, certainly not without some American ges-
ture towards the Palestinians. If it were the oil, it came at a
very high price. In the first year, the U.S. was budgeting for a
$100 billion for the Iraq operation, with an expected return of
less than one tenth of that in oil revenues, which would have
to go to Iraq anyway. And one year after the invasion, gaso-
line and oil prices were at their highest in thirty years, with
OPEC, led by the Saudis who had been repeatedly snubbed
by the administration, reducing production.

As the rhetoric built up in the summer of 2002, Richard
Murphy of the Council on Foreign Relations commented presciently that the president "is a believer. This is a man who's

on a mission. He is very evangelical about terrorism: he's got to root out evil. I wonder if in his mind there really *is* a very strong linkage between Saddam Hussein and al-Qaeda. Evil is there, and evil must be uprooted and the fixation on terrorism has now encompassed Saddam Hussein—who 'tried to kill my father' as a footnote. Bush seems to think the facts are there about the linkage—if only we could discover them. In his mind they are joined up. He does not speak as man with any doubts."

In fact, Murphy called it right. That September, Bush the Younger actually said it in a speech about Saddam Hussein in Houston: "There's no doubt he can't stand us, after all, this is the guy that tried to kill my Dad at one time." Suspecting that most Americans, let alone the rest of the world, might not be tempted to risk Armageddon for a Bush family feud, a "senior White House official" rushed to comment that the president "doesn't want to appear to personalize" the U.S. campaign against Saddam. He explained that the intended victim of the assassination plot "happens to be the president's father, but the important part is he's a former president of the United States. There is some question, in fact, whether or not the alleged assassination attempt against his dad back in 1993 may not have been an expedient invention of the same imaginative Kuwaitis who had tried to frame a guilty man by accusing Saddam Hussein's troops of emptying out Kuwaiti incubators.

So there we have the explanations for why, almost at the beginning of the war against the Taliban and Osama bin Laden, President George W. Bush effectively broke off from the engagement and went after Saddam Hussein.

Does it all come back to "family, friends, and faith"? He really may want to ingratiate himself with the alpha male of the Bush clan—his father—and get closure for all the times he feels he has not lived up to patriarchal expectations by getting the man who tried to kill his dad. He may even think his Texas friends want him to go after the oil, although none of the major oil companies are so theologically nice as to worry about who they buy their product from. Certainly his friends in the administration, except for Colin Powell, were pushing for the Iraq thing. And finally, almost as disturbingly as any deep psychological impulses from his relationship with his father, Bush really does see the world as a Manichaean struggle between absolute evil—as in axis of—and good—himself. Of course it helps to have apostles like Lt. Gen. William G. Boykin, deputy undersecretary of defense for intelligence in charge of operations against al-Qaeda, who has claimed that "we are in the Army of God" and that the president was "appointed by God."

Apart from Colin Powell, Boykin is perhaps one of the few genuinely inspired and clever appointments made by Bush the Younger—if we accept the premise of setting a fundamentalist to catch one.

The one excuse for the war that we can be sure had no weight whatsoever with Bush was Saddam Hussein's lack of cooperation with the United Nations inspectors, who the Pentagon intellectuals had, after all, consistently derided for years. As we saw with the invocation of Iraqi aggression against Iran, and indeed in his wallowings over his National Guard absence, it was a case of any excuse in a pickle.

The president was simply pandering to people like Colin Powell and Tony Blair—and indeed the U.S. Congress—who wanted an excuse before they followed the global commander in chief into possible Armageddon. Because his father had been U.S. ambassador to the UN, he was perhaps slightly less inclined to dismiss the institution than his sneering administration members in the Pentagon and in Cheney's entourage, but only slightly. When he was among friends, in Texas, for example, he let his mask slip to reveal the same contempt.

So he was prepared to go the UN route, not least because Powell and Blair had told him this was the price for getting allies on board, not least, as it turned out, the Turks, whose territory, it had been assumed, was to be the staging post for at least one wing of the invasion.

But then, after a lot of huffing and puffing, there came the nightmare scenario. Saddam began to cooperate, and by January 2003, the inspectors were in, and what is more, finding out, as much to their own surprise as anyone else's, that he did not have any prohibited weapons after all, despite effectively bluffing everyone for years that he did.

By then, Bush had set a deadline of mid-March 2003 for the invasion to start. The official excuse was that after that, the desert heat would start proving too much for the troops already in place. Air conditioners may have been one solution, but they would not have cooled down the fever heat of righteousness anger in the commander in chief. He had the faith: this was the war he wanted, and this was when he wanted it.

Even his chum Blair tried to persuade him to try a few

weeks extension, but British officials report that the president was obdurate. The date was unchangeable, even if it did mean no UN endorsement and no opening up of the Turkish route, and even if it meant fewer reinforcements, and fewer forces for the assault. Maybe it was stubbornness, a determination to show that once a commander in chief has made up his mind, that's it. Who knows? It may have been a case of overcompensation for the insecurity that he may feel in his more lucid moments. Despite the bluster, the uniforms, and the title, in his heart he must know that he actually skipped direct participation in the real war of his generation, and he was about to unleash the scourge of war on a succeeding generation.

17 NEGLECTING THE TROOPS

WHILE PARADING HIMSELF IN uniform on almost every occasion, and basking in the adulation due the commander in chief, George Bush has neglected the most elementary point of military leadership: he has not looked after the welfare and safety of his men and women.

Leaving aside the question of whether the Iraq war should have been fought at all, we move on to the question of how, it were done at all, it should have been conducted.

Military intelligence has become an oxymoron since the weapons of mass destruction debacle, because Bush the Younger's minions in the Pentagon, whose military experience was in most cases even less than his, were empowered to plot the conduct of the war.

Their bedrock assumptions were wrong. Firstly, there were no massive stockpiles of chemical and biological, let alone nuclear, weapons waiting to greet the invading forces, which is just as well really, since there were not nearly enough American troops to cope with that threat if it had become real, not least since the Pentagon's other assumption, of massive defections by the Iraqi army and uprisings by the Shi'a didn't happen either.

Under Clinton, the Pentagon was run by the military, and the only time it showed signs of aggression was about its budget. Madeline Albright actually asked Colin Powell when he was general what we needed all these armed forces for if we can't use them. Clinton, more sensitive than Bush about his lack of military experience, let the professional military have far too much influence, not only over the Pentagon, but over administration policy all together.

Unsurprisingly, the Bush administration, who neither individually nor collectively evoke sensitivity in the mind of the beholder, had no such compunctions. Their civilian appointees regularly override the professional military.

To begin with, Bush and Rumsfeld, by insisting that the attack on Iraq go ahead in mid-March regardless, not only took bigger risks than their own military commanders wanted, by sending in a smaller force, with insufficient reinforcements, but skimped on their equipment.

The army, with some experience in these things, wanted four hundred thousand troops. Firstly, they wanted to prepare for eventualities, not even unexpected ones but those WMDs that they did expect, but were unexpectedly absent; secondly, they wanted to secure the country in the ensuing occupation. The Bush administration wanted a small mobile

force, working more as a catalyst for the quasi–coup d'état
that their Iraqi National Congress friends, like Ahmed Cha-
labi, had persuaded them was going to happen.

The actual military commanders were haggled and bullied
into halving the troop numbers, with holdout Chief of Staff
Eric Shinseki being publicly putdown by Paul Wolfowitz as
"wildly off the mark," for suggesting that it would take several hundred thousand troops to occupy the country.

As a result of this interference by know-all chickenhawks,
the army that went in was small, with thousands of unused,
and in the immediate period unusable, troops strewn across
the world, from those still in the U.S. and Germany, to those
who were waiting in the Mediterranean to go through Turkey.
Missing in action were the armor and artillery as well.

That was partly the result of the tactical decisions on force
composition by the Pentagon civilians appointed by Bush,
whose bravery knows no limits when sending other people
into the fray. It was also a consequence of the commander in
chief's insistence that the attack be launched in March, come
what may, regardless of the UN and regardless of the Turks
and others.

The operation was, in the short-term, a quick success. In
the long-term, it is killing both doctors and patients in large
numbers, as we shall see when we look at the casualty figures
from the occupation.

We should give due credit to the one major factor in the
speed and success of the operation. The Pentagon and the
White House were completely wrong about Iraqi possession
of weapons of mass destruction, and although they are still

gnashing their teeth in frustration and denying the self-evident truth, the rest of us, not least the American and British forces who actually had to go in, should be very glad that they were wrong.

As for the looting and consequent problems of the occupation, they were not just predictable: *they were predicted*. The State Department study, discarded by the Pentagon, and the actual military's contingency plans, equally suppressed by the foolhardier type of Pentagon intellectual, all wanted more troops precisely for that reason.

Despite every serious study warning of the need to assert authority and stop the type of looting that took place, the Pentagon not only disregarded the possibility, it issued no orders to its overstretched forces on what to do.

Actually, Rumsfeld had a point about using fewer troops. The U.S. Army did not really have enough troops to fight the wars that the commander in chief was waging. To run the invasion-lite force that emerged from the compromise between the actual military and the Pentagon produced several highly ironic results. To begin with, specialized combat units were pulled away from the hunt for bin Laden in Afghanistan, which is a very strange way to wage a war on terror intended to be payback for September 11.

In the context of the commander in chief's own military career, the other, surely unintended irony was that an unprecedented number of National Guard men and women found themselves called up and dropped off in the desert.

18 GIVE US THE TOOLS, WE'LL FINISH THE JOB

A GOOD COMMANDER MAKES sure that his men have the wherewithal to fight and win. "Republicans like weapons systems; Democrats like the soldiers," General Wesley Clark has said, pithily and accurately. In fact, he could have gone further. These Republicans like weapons-systems *makers* and their lobbyists. Rumsfeld and Bush, before and after September 11, starved low-tech high-manpower agencies that could actually have an effect on terrorism in favor of "Star Wars"–style missile-defense systems. The response to a relatively low-tech airplane hijacking was to put money into space-based systems and missile interceptions.

For years, these tests had been shooting dollars into space. Sixty billion dollars had already been spent before September 11 and $6 billion more are currently earmarked for the Strategic Defense Initiative and its various sequels. In fact, after twenty years and a steady hemorrhaging of dollars—

mostly to the aerospace companies who were involved in inventing the threat and the concept—SDI technology has advanced to the point where, if a fish is very large, brightly dyed, and nailed to the bottom of barrel, sharpshooters with a double-barreled shotgun may occasionally hit it, assuming there are no other fish around to distract them.

The only unequivocally successful test of the technology, back in 1984, was achieved by turning the target on its side so it appeared bigger, and heating it up so that it was brighter, to make it easier for the intercepting missile to hit. Scrutiny, from the General Accounting Office (GAO), revealed that other tests involved targets containing charges with explosives that would be detonated if the interceptors got anywhere near them.

Real missiles would come in swarms, surrounded by decoys and debris, and are somewhat coyer about showing their best side to would-be anti-missile defenses. And terrorists come in airliners, laden with fuel and passengers.

While there seems to be an open-ended budget for hardware, Rumsfeld has strong ideas about the military and is riding roughshod over the sensibilities of military officers. In contrast to the billions aerospace contractors are getting, the actual troops, in particular the National Guardsmen, are suffering from some serious shortages.

A "Lessons Learned" report from the military reported that, "Soldiers still spend too much of their own money to purchase the quality packs, pouches, belts, underwear, socks, and gloves they believe they need for mission success." One serving soldier's mother ran up $1,000 on her Visa card outfitting her departing warrior.

But having a clean pair of shorts is one thing. A more lethal and persistent complaint has been personal armor. In an occupation that has hostile snipers hanging out of every palm tree, there is a lethal lottery in play. Which of the troops gets body armor?

Persistent reports indicate that those at the back of the line for the most up to date versions are reservists and National Guardsman. It is almost as if First Lieutenant George W. Bush had had to fly his F-102 with a parachute that he knew would not work once he was in the air.

Across the country, the families of soldiers have been holding bake sales and other cozily domestic fund-raisers to buy this essential equipment for their relatives posted to Iraq. The dilemma was typically acute for the 1032nd Transportation Company, a unit of the Virginia National Guard who, unlike their president, had not managed to evade hazardous overseas duty.

The men and women of the unit were at the real front line, driving trucks in convoy along the miles of Iraqi highways, along extended supply lines between Baghdad and Nasriyah. The trucks, without protection, made them sitting ducks for the local snipers, who were after all not supposed to be there sniping, since the Pentagon assumed that the only resistance was from infiltrating fundamentalists. The National Guardsmen had clocked up 2.3 million miles with no dead when the *Washington Post* got hold of their story.[46]

Remarkably, the first three-quarters of those miles were clocked up with no body armor, at least none issued by the Pentagon. The *Post* reported on a Kalashnikov bullet fired from a passing BMW, which slammed into the chest of Specialist Nathan Williams. All that came between his heart and the lethal projectile was a contraption that could have been used by a medieval knight, a $3 plate of quarter-inch steel slotted into the Kevlar shrapnel vest, carved out in their Virginia base's workshop.

Luckier later arrivals had state-of-the-art boron carbide ceramic vests designed to stop high-velocity bullets. The shortage of body armor became a natural issue in the battle between the former member of Yale's Davenport Armour Council and the Democrats. The former could have recycled metal beer kegs, one presumes. Bush's campaign ads with their customary chutzpah have been on the offensive, accusing Kerry of voting against the bill that would finance armor.

By the time that the 1032nd were issued with standard armor in January this year, their actual transportation job had been taken over by Halliburton subsidiary Kellogg Brown & Root, which had, doubtless with tort insurance on their mind, made sure all their drivers were properly equipped with the latest armor.

Even a year after the invasion, Baghdad-bound troops had heard it on the grapevine that if you did not want to be shot, you bought your own armor, and did not trust the Pentagon's promises that it would be on hand when needed. It can cost several thousand dollars a set, but draftees to Iraq are canny about the promises of their civilian bosses.

Bulletproofme.com in Texas (where else?) has sold two hundred sets at $1,200 per vest to departing soldiers. The Pentagon, one year after, is now buying twenty-five thousand a month from other suppliers—who charge $1,500, but there are still not enough for each GI out in Iraq to have one each. Once again, it appears that it is the reservists who are at the back of the line for the equipment.

Vietnam-era flak jackets and armor-free Humvees are what they say they are issued when they go to the front. Staff Sgt. Dave Harris wrote a letter to *Stars and Stripes* telling how his comrade, Mike Quinn, died in the Sunni Triangle. Quinn's unit was one that did not have enough vests to go 'round, so he gave his to a younger man. The bullet that killed Quinn went unimpeded on its way.

Soldiers' families wrote to Congress about the deadly lottery that ensues when there are only thirty up-to-date vests for 120 soldiers. The modern ones not only stop high-velocity bullets, they are one-third the weight of the old ones, which is no mean advantage in the heart of Iraq.

While the Bush campaign attacked Kerry for not voting for the president's $87 billion Halliburton assistance bill, by the summer of 2004, it was the White House playing coy. Pentagon sources all pointed out that the money was already pretty much spent. But there are higher priorities than winning wars—such as winning elections. Going back for more money for a war that was supposed to be won and over, with only months to go to the election was not going to look good and would have allowed the Democrats to counter-attack.

The Bush budget for the financial year beginning October 2004 did not include any Iraq spending and his officials did not anticipate a request until the new calendar year—January 2005. However, the administration forgot to consult the

Iraqis, who in Fallujah and elsewhere were vociferously disputing the victory that the commander in chief had declared a year before on the decks of the USS *Abraham Lincoln*.

The results were an ample validation for Wesley Clark's statement about the president's sensitivities to the needs of ordinary soldiers. By April the army's public needs list for things to improve the comfort and survivability of the troops included $132 million for bolt-on vehicle armor; $879 million for combat helmets, silk-weight underwear, boots and other clothing; $21.5 million for M249 squad automatic weapons; and $27 million for ammunition magazines, night sights and ammo packs. They also wanted another $956 million for repairing desert-damaged equipment and $102 million to replace equipment lost in combat. All of these items had been squeezed out of the defense budget, perhaps because GI's don't and can't lobby Congress or raise campaign contributions on the same scale as the manufacturers of more spectacular and expensive equipment.

Tellingly, the Marine Corps's request for $40 million for body armor, lightweight helmets and other equipment for "marines engaged in the global war on terrorism," went out the window. They also wanted 1,800 squad automatic weapons and 5,400 M4 carbine rifles.

Another big issue was the Humvees and similar vehicles that TV viewers saw regularly in flames on the streets of Iraqi towns. So confident were they of being greeted as liberators, and pelted with nothing more lethal than bouquets, the Pentagon sent in hundreds of unarmored vehicles. It was so serious that, unprecedentedly, even Israel had to take a back seat, and in April, the Pentagon diverted to Iraq 120 armored Humvees purchased by the IDF, while announcing a $110 million contract for still more of them.

Even Congressman Curt Weldon, a Pennsylvania Republican who was vice chair of the House Armed Services Committee, called the administration's defense budget request "outrageous" and "immoral." "There needs to be a supplemental, whether it's a presidential election year or not," he said. "The support of our troops has to be the number one priority of this country. . . . Somebody's got to get serious about this." [47]

Serious for him was $10 billion but even that seemed to be an underestimate. However, there was no sign that the president who does not have to explain himself to others was going to break under the strain. It was unlikely that there would be any supplemental hostage to fortune until after the election and the next round of terminological inexactitudes.

19 STICKY ENDS

THOSE WHO FORESAW a sticky end for the war in Iraq were right in one, perverse, way. American firearms issued to troops have always been notoriously high maintenance, certainly compared with the ubiquitous and almost indestructible AK47s wielded by so many of its opponents.

To compound that error, despite Colin Powell's famous allegation that "we do deserts, not mountains," the lubricant issued to troops to clean and maintain their weapons in Iraq has been accused of being totally inappropriate, collecting sand and dust and causing them to jam.

The Pentagon report on the incident that put Private Jessica Lynch in the headlines says that many of the soldiers involved in the ambush had "weapons malfunctions." Indeed, Private Lynch herself reported, "When we were told to lock and load—that's when my weapon jammed." As a result, ten of her colleagues in the 507th Army Maintenance

Company had terminal life malfunctions. They died in a hail of crossfire.

Thrashing around to keep Lynch as an expedient show-biz hero, the Pentagon blamed "inadequate individual maintenance," for the debacle in the ambush, alleging that the GIs had not cleaned their weapons. However, many more objective sources say that the fault lies in the lubricant that they were ordered to use.

Reports back on lessons learned say soldiers repeatedly stated that the official-issue lubricant "was not a good choice for weapon maintenance," claiming it "attracted sand to the weapon." It added, "Soldiers considered a product called MiliTec to be a much better solution for lubricating." Indeed, soldiers wrote home to relatives asking them to send it. In the meantime, the more canny among them used condoms to protect their weapons, which would give the moral majority supporters of the war something to chew on.

However, Bush's and Rumsfeld's Pentagon had actually cancelled all military purchase orders for the commercially produced lube, MiliTec, at the start of the war, until October, which was too late for Sgt. Don Walters, and the ten of his comrades of the 507th Army Maintenance Company killed in the ambush. The Pentagon posthumously and belatedly awarded a Silver Star to Walters this March, after a campaign by his mother backed by other survivors. His actions in fighting to the death had previously been attributed to Jessica Lynch, desperate as the Pentagon was for a photogenic, live heroine, despite her own protestations that she had not fired a shot, since her gun had jammed as had those of her comrades.

An earlier report in the *Washington Post* on April 14, 2003, had contained the first detailed accounts of the ambush from the just-rescued POWs:

> The bullets and explosions came from all sides. Some of the vehicles flipped over. Other drivers hit the gas hoping to outrun the danger, but ran into even heavier fire. In the swirling dust, soldiers' rifles jammed. Pfc. Patrick Miller, 23, from suburban Wichita, began shoving rounds into his rifle one at a time, firing single shots at enemies swarming all around. Finally, it fell to Sgt. James Riley, a 31-year-old bachelor from Pennsauken, N.J., and the senior soldier present, to surrender. "We were like Custer," he recalled today, still sounding shocked. "We were surrounded. We had no working weapons. We couldn't even make a bayonet charge. We would have been mowed down."[48]

20 VOLUNTEERS OF AMERICA

SINCE THE WAR IN Iraq got underway in 2003, at least 53,693 out of nearly 460,000 National Guard members had been mobilized one year later. A year after the president had declared victory, they and the reserves between them made up almost half the garrison there. When Ted Kennedy complained during the debate on the president's $87 billion request, thirteen thousand had been on active duty for a year, and many of them groused as they were rotated out to Iraq as fast as they were rotated home from Afghanistan.

Rumsfeld has fought a battle in the Pentagon for smaller, more effective, combat forces, and his and the commander in chief's prejudices against using real U.S. soldiers for "nation-building" feed into this. The game plan was for the U.S. to get in, win, and let the Indians, Pakistanis, Turks, and the like come in and do the garrisoning. It is reminiscent of the way that the Germans used Ukrainians and the Japanese used

Korean troops as prison-camp guards in World War II. It was singularly ineffective in Afghanistan as we have seen, but while no one in Washington really cares if that falls apart, the spillover from Iraq is frightening, sitting as it is in close proximity to the world's biggest oil deposits.

When the diplomatic ineptitude of the commander in chief, helped in no small measure by the rebarbative comments of the defense secretary about sundry foreigners, ensured that none of these latter-day Sepoy divisions were available, he put in the National Guard and reservists.

Naturally, since he does not regard them as front-line warriors in the war on terror, they get hand-me-down equipment, even though of course, in reality, any U.S. military in Iraq is on the front line. Their night-vision goggles are leftovers from Vietnam, but Vietnam is in their vision in other ways.

Under stop-loss orders, some forty thousand troops, including sixteen thousand reservists and National Guardsmen, have been effectively conscripted. They thought they were about to finish their term but have been told that they are retained in the service whether they like it or not. Their listed termination date on their paycheck is now 2030—which is the the payroll department's way of saying, "Whenever." This used to be called the draft, but it is now being done through the back-door.

Stop-loss orders were first used in recent times by none other than then Secretary of Defense Richard B. Cheney in the first Gulf War, which of course has its own irony—the timely pregnancy of his wife which allowed him to dodge serving in Vietnam.

In fact, it may be illegal as well as immoral. Congress, which is supposed to keep the commander in chief in check, set a manpower limit of 480,000 for the U.S. Army, but this insidious backdoor conscription has raised numbers to 500,000, and that is still not enough to meet the demands placed upon them by the warlord in the White House.

In an October 9, 2003, speech to the Air National Guard and reserve troops at Pease Air Force Base in New Hampshire, the president flattered them by telling them that they had become part of the backbone of the military.

"Citizen-soldiers are serving in every front on the war on terror," Bush said. "And you're making your state and your country proud." He cited "people like Master Sergeant Jake Negrotti, of Plaistow, New Hampshire . . . a member of the New Hampshire Air National Guard. He's volunteered for overseas deployments three times since September the eleventh. He served in Pakistan, Afghanistan, and Iraq."

One wonders if the disloyal thought crossed anyone's mind that not all members of the Air National Guard were historically so eager to volunteer for overseas duty. At least on this merciful occasion he did not refer to himself as commander in chief—or wear a uniform. However, making the country proud was not enough for many reservists and National Guardsmen who, having, unlike Bush, served the full term of their engagement, wanted out, only to discover that the regulations that let the lucky few out earlier, can keep the unlucky in later.

Some reservists who had been transferred into active duty units had noticed that while the professionals had been rotated home, they had remained in Baghdad. That has apparently been a common complaint among guards and reservists. The regular army feels that the part-timers have been on a gravy train and should take the rough with the smooth now they are called to active duty. It is understandable—but ironic that no one applied it to the commander in chief in similar circumstances.

Counterproductively, the stop-loss orders along with continuous duty overseas cause resentment which makes it more likely that those who can will not reenlist afterwards.

The army conducted its own polls of personnel in Iraq, after a rash of suicides. More than half—52 percent of them—admitted that their own morale was low, while 70 percent of them thought that their colleague's morale was low—which may be a more accurate assessment of their own feelings. Almost 75 percent of those polled assessed that "their battalion-level command leadership was poor" and showed "a lack of concern" for their soldiers. And that was after only six months of the occupation. More revealingly, and not surprisingly, being in a lower rank and being in a reserve unit enhanced the gloom. The unprecedented survey was completed in October—a mere four months after the commander in chief had announced the end of the war.

One cause for low morale could, of course, be poor pay. According to a military salary survey by Chicago outplacement firm Challenger, Gray & Christmas, a private with one year of service has a base pay of $15,480 a year, which compares barely favorably with the $14,144 for child-care workers and movie ushers, and the $15,080 earned by crossing guards in 2002, according to the Bureau of Labor Statistics. A corporal with three years of service will get $19,980 annually, while, proving that the army is socialism in practice with its low differentials, a newly commissioned officer with George W. Bush's rank would only get $26,200 a year—with no guarantee of a Bush-style family trust fund to back it up.

As a big concession the 2005 Bush budget proposes that the combat pay will not count toward eligibility for food stamps—for which twenty-five thousand military families are eligible.

But a recent GAO report also brought out yet another problem. Low pay or not, it is useful to get it and while the National Guard is quick to send out mobilization notices, it is notoriously slow to send payment. The GAO cited, "Four Virginia Special Forces soldiers who were injured in Afghanistan and unable to resume their civilian jobs experienced problems in receiving entitled active duty pay and related healthcare."

With blood and irony however, market forces, the beloved panacea of George W. Bush, are bringing an odd equilibrium to the situation. The absence of the several hundred thousand troops that the military, probably correctly assessed as necessary to secure a restive Iraq, has created a market opportunity for free enterprise.

Private security firms are moving in, and since they cannot rely on stop-loss orders, they have offered high pay and good conditions, like sixty days on duty followed by sixty days leave. Who have they offered it to? Experienced military types who are dropping out of the military to earn double or quadruple pay—and still keep their military pensions. In April, it was estimated that there were over 20,000 private "security" officers.

Short of contracting out the whole of the Pentagon to Halliburton however, which may not sound too outlandish to some of the think tanks that the administration listens to now, the commander in chief is unlikely to divert the steady flow of tax dollars from hardware contractors to the actual soldiers.

Over the ten years up to 2002, 7,500 business executives took—it is hard to "earned" about such figures—$177 billion in remuneration. That would have paid one-third of the payroll for the forces over that period.

No wonder, then that the *Army Times* thundered in an editorial, sounding more like the *Socialist Worker* than a military journal,[49] that while the Bush administration could find seeming limitless funds for tax cuts aimed at the rich, "They can't seem to find time to make progress on minor tax provision that would be a boon to military homeowners, reservists who travel long distances for training, and parents deployed to combat zones among others." Even, it complained, one of the tax provisions easing residency rules of service members to qualify for capital-gains exemption when selling a home, had been stalled in the corridors of power for five years.

In the army as in civilian life, lower ranks would have their pay raises capped at 2 percent while higher ranks got more.

On housing the *Army Times* mentioned the cuts in the military construction bill for "crumbling military housing and other facilities," and spoke approvingly of David Obey (D-Wisconsin) who wanted to restore a billion of it by reducing the tax handout to those who earned more than a million from $83,500 a year to $83,300. The Republicans on the appropriations committee had no difficulty whatsoever voting it down. No one has yet produced a U.S. military person earning more than a million a year from the Pentagon, at least, so it is a clear demonstration of the priorities. In similar vein, the administration tried to close down commissaries, where military families can get cheap supplies, and military base schools.

Bush and his team clearly suspect what others have said, that with its subsidized housing, free schooling, and free health care, in a strange way, the military shows that social democracy can work. They want to make it stop!

However, whether it reflects the reality or not, the Republican self-perception that it can treat the military as a vote bank does have consequences. They can be scared off some of their crazier and meaner plans in ways that less-courted groups cannot.

When Bush announced he was going to veto a bill that allowed veterans to collect disability pay and pensions simultaneously, he had to back down under pressure from GOP lawmakers whose constituents forced them go onto the side of the Democrats.

The same fear of being out-militarized on the Left led enough Republicans to back the Democrats against a presidential veto when the commander in chief, fresh from giving hundreds of billions in tax relief to the richest Americans, proposed cutting combat pay from $225 to $150 a month, and the family separation allowance from $250 to $100. Most callously of all, the commander in chief who had ducked a war that killed forty thousand American military, and just started another that had killed approaching seven hundred, threatened to veto a proposal to double the $6,000 gratuity for relatives of killed soldiers.

In 2003, the White House cavalierly thought that these types of payments were "wasteful and unnecessary," adjectives which many people might apply both to the separations, the combat, and the deaths that led to such payments.

As the *Army Times* editorial concluded, "President Bush and the Republican-controlled Congress have missed no opportunity to heap richly deserved praise on the military. But talk is cheap and getting cheaper by the day, judging by the nickel-and-dime treatment the troops are getting lately."

But in 2004, with an election pending, military votes in the balance, and, no doubt the *Army Times* editorial ringing in its ears, the administration changed its mind and agreed to support the payments.

21 THEN AND NOW WITH THE GUARD

IT IS INTERESTING TO compare what happens to National Guardsmen now, with the treatment once accorded the commander in chief. When Lieutenant George W. Bush was the same age as Staff Sgt. Camilo Mejia he would occasionally turn up at air force bases across the South, to sign up for drill, or not, or to take medical examinations, or not, as the fancy took him. Sergeant Mejia turned up at Fort Stewart in Georgia on March 17, 2004, to hand himself in. After he reported to the air base, military police released the sergeant with written orders to report to his unit, in Miami.

In October 2003, he had returned home to Florida on leave from his National Guard unit based in Iraq and decided that he could not return. This was the first large-scale leave program of the war and the *Washington Post* reported that out of one thousand three hundred participants, thirty had not shown up for the return. It cited several of them who gave reasons much less ideological than Sergeant Mejia.[50]

He did not return for duty, since, he said, the time out had given him time to think about what he and his comrades were working on. "I am saying no to war. I went to Iraq and was an instrument of violence, and now I have decided to become an instrument of peace." The number of civilians being killed in Iraq persuaded him that that was not, in reality, his role. Tod Ensign, a lawyer and director of Citizen Soldier, a New York veterans organization commented, "They don't want us there; we don't want to be there," he said. "We're getting killed there."

Mejia sought conscientious-objector status, but lawyers said he would have difficulty. Conscientious objectors are considered to be those against all wars, and it is difficult to establish the status by concentrating on the way one war was conceived or waged.

Lieutenant Colonel Ron Tittle, spokesman for the Florida National Guard, said Mejia was given leave last year. His company tried to reach him in March after he failed to report for duty. After weeks of worrying about what to do, the army decided to charge him for his five months' desertion—and worried about how long it would take to get a court-martial up and running. But they were alert to the essentials, restricting him to the Fort Stewart base, and prohibiting face-to-face interviews with the media. He was AWOL for less than half the time that George W. Bush was missing, but importantly, Mejia had no known family-, friend-, or faith-based links to high-ranking politicians.

With rare sensitivity, the military is not sending out press gangs or snatch squads of MPs after disgruntled nonreturnees.

The Fort Bragg Base in North Carolina (and yes, it is named after a Confederate general) claims to have assembled a "team to capture deserters." But 108 of the absentees that have been grabbed since September 11, 2001, were arrested by the civil police and only nine by the military.

Interestingly, just as Mejia was returning from Iraq, UPI reported that the army was responding to complaints and sending doctors to Fort Stewart to help hundreds of invalid soldiers there, including many who had returned from Iraq.

National Guard and Army Reserve troops had been waiting for weeks and months on "medical hold," "warehoused in rows of spare, steamy and dark cement barracks in a sandy field" where they had to walk or hobble on crutches to a nearby communal latrine where, UPI reported, they have "propped office partitions between otherwise open toilets for privacy. . . . Showering is in a communal, cinder-block room. Soldiers say they have to buy their own toilet paper." Around 250 of the 600 were returnees from Iraq.

The purpose of "medical hold" is for the army to decide how sick or disabled the troops are, and what benefits they may be due. When UPI went in, for a period from October 14 to, ironically, Veterans Day, November 11, there were no more doctors' appointments available. Despite the insalubrious conditions, the commander in chief was charging troops under treatment at hospitals like Fort Stewart $8.10 a day for their food—at least we presume he takes responsibility for his subordinates—until word got out.

Congressmen from both sides of the house shoehorned a provision to lift the charges on troops wounded, injured, or who become ill while in combat zone or on hazardous duty in the president's $87 billion Iraqi war budget, backdated until September 11, 2001. While the relief was only temporary, it was due for renewal September 30, 2004. These dates are deeply significant. Congress had to invoke September 11 to force through an elementary act of fairness and kindness— and it may yet be renewed by a hitherto reluctant commander in chief because September 30 is just before the general election.

Several of the National Guard and Army Reserve soldiers suspected that the way they were being treated at Fort Stewart was because the army was trying push them out with reduced benefits for the ailments that service overseas gave them.

Once again there was that familiar complaint that that the regular active duty personnel were getting far better treatment. Yes, things had changed since First Lieutenant George W. Bush was in the guard. He knew all the tricks and loopholes, but as commander in chief, he was not going to let anyone else get away with it.

22 WELL DONE THOU GOOD AND FAITHFUL SERVANT—NOW GET LOST

HOW MANY CASUALTIES HAVE there been in Iraq? It is a simple question, but there seemed to be a willful refusal on the part of the administration to find out, or make the figures available. There are occasional inspired and inspiring stories about the brave amputees who want to go back into the fray for more. But how many of them are there?

At the beginning of April, the Defense Department's casualty report claims 2,988 were wounded in action, during Operation Iraqi Freedom, of whom 1,910 were not back in action in three days. But the week before, the Pentagon had told Congress that there had been 18,004 medical evacuations from Iraq by then.[51]

In January, the U.S. Army alone had admitted to NPR that there had been 8,848 soldiers evacuated from Iraq. The air force, navy, and marines were included in the suspiciously low Department of Defense casualty reports. Something did not not add up, obviously. Senator Chuck Hagel (R-Nebraska), a Vietnam veteran himself, told NPR in January 2004, that he had requested "the total number of American battlefield casualties in Afghanistan and Iraq." He had also asked, "What is the official Pentagon definition of wounded in action? What is the procedure for releasing this information in a timely way to the public?"

After six weeks, the Pentagon wrote back: "At this time we were unfortunately lacking in information, and we didn't have the information you requested." Consider the likelihood of that. The most expensive, sophisticated military machine in the world was "unable" to produce the statistics on losses in the war, while publishing a clearly imaginary, and equally clearly low number for the public.

Shakespeare's contemporary, John Webster, wrote of the ten thousand several ways that death has for men to make their exits. It seems that at least that many have been evacuated in ways that are beneath the Pentagon's notice. Senator Max Cleland (D-Georgia), who in Vietnam lost three limbs when a grenade went off, would not have appeared in these laundered numbers. Nor would the hundreds of men and women bitten by sand flies (there is a lot of sand) who developed leishmaniasis, nor those who have complained of nonspecific ailments.

At the beginning of April, some of those were almost diagnosed, thanks to the tabloid *New York Daily News*, which paid for tests on nine members of the 442nd Military Police Company of the New York Army National Guard for depleted uranium contamination. The company usually recruits New

York City cops, firefighters, and correction officers—groups that tend to be influential and active in political affairs. Four of them tested positive, which at least got them some attention from a Pentagon that tends to think that one of the benefits of the National Guard is that its members suffer off-site where they can usually be ignored. The army ordered tests on all members of the unit at Fort Dix but the rest of the unit was returned from Iraq later in April. They swamped the testing facilities.

The administration is not just concerned about the numbers. It is also concerned about the individuals, in its own perverse way. Citing privacy concerns, the Walter Reed military hospital banned Disabled American Veterans, a congressional-chartered organization, from entering to speak to the wounded being treated there.

DAV Executive Director David W. Gorman complained to Rumsfeld in January 2004, saying, "With combat casualties returning to military hospitals in the United States, it is essential that these wounded soldiers, sailors, airmen, and marines be made fully aware of their rights, benefits, and health-care options even before they leave military service."

But the group was caught in a classic catch-22: the military would only allow them in to meet patients who requested to meet them, but citing privacy, it would not allow the DAV to know who was in the wards to let them know what help it could offer!

Quite whose privacy was under discussion here was not clear, since the group did not want access to the medical records. But it does give advice to wounded veterans on how to steer their way through the labyrinthine defense bureaucracy and, more crucially, it had offered unwelcome and public advice to the commander in chief on the administration's treatment of veterans. This is dangerous stuff in election year, when, as we saw, First Lt. Bush, Rtd., was making his military credentials a key issue in the fight against Kerry.

Significantly, other veterans' organizations, which had been less critical of the Pentagon, seemed to have no problems. Without actually accusing the administration of political skullduggery—perish the thought—DAV spokesman Dave Autry did speculate, "The question that we have been asked many times is, 'What's really behind this?'" He asked, "Is it that they don't want people to know the cost of this war in blood and in treasure? We don't have an answer to that question."

23 VETERANS AND THE ADMINISTRATION

"A MAN WHO IS good enough to shed his blood for his country is good enough to be given a square deal afterwards," declared Teddy Roosevelt,[52] who may have been even more bellicose than George W. Bush, but whose private militia was raised with the express intention of going to fight. We are entitled to doubt whether cutting the Veterans Benefits Administration hospital service, and slashing benefits to veterans would count as a "square deal"!

The commander in chief, when not strutting the boards in uniform, sits down in a suit and calculates petty ways to save money. There is a complete disconnect between his posed role as a "retired military person or veteran," and the way he actually treats his co-opted comrades in arms. His administration's behavior is like that of a toddler who hides behind the drapes and cannot understand how people can see his feet sticking out from under them.

In 2003, while he was planning for wars that would certainly increase the demand for the services of the Veterans Administration hospitals, he cut their budgets by $3 billion. He fought off an attempt by congressmen on both sides of the house to add $1.3 billion of the $87 billion to the hospitals. The White House, a.k.a. the commander in chief, also proposed a $250 co-payment for veterans who have so-called "priority eight" ailments, those that are supposed to be nonservice related.

The cuts provoked even Ronald Conley, commander of the conservative American Legion, who declared that "this is a raw deal for veterans no matter how you cut it. The administration is sending a message that these vets are not a priority at all."

We should not be too surprised. Bush is continuing in his expected patrician tradition: the one that lionizes "our boys" in abstract, when they go to war, but despises them and locks them up for vagabonds and hoboes when they are demobilized. Another more sympathetic patrician, Benjamin Disraeli, Britain's first Jewish prime minister, wrote, "The services in wartime are fit only for desperadoes but in peace are fit only for fools."

The present commander in chief was, of course, a peacetime soldier, a summer soldier and sunshine patriot, who has little thought for those in the winter of the lives at Walter Reed and similar places. He could be foolish as well, as the election approaches and more and more in the military begin to question why a Republican draft dodger should be seen as their automatic choice for president—and, oh yes, commander in chief.

24 BECAUSE OUR PRESIDENT LIED

RUDYARD KIPLING WAS NOT just bombastic. His suggested epitaph for the fallen was:

> If any question why we died,
> Tell them, because our fathers lied.

As this book was being finished, the mayhem in Fallujah brought the total dead to over seven hundred, more than three quarters of them killed since commander in chief, First Lieutenant, Rtd., and naval aviator George W. Bush had landed on the USS *Abraham Lincoln* to announce victory. While we are unsure of the figures for the wounded, and the final total for the dead, we can be sure of one thing: not even this White House will be crass enough to use clips from that tasteless display of braggadocio for its already crass enough campaign commercials.

We have to ask, why was it that President Bill Clinton was so scared of casualties that he almost lost at least one war, in Kosovo, because of it, and almost abandoned the operation in Haiti. It was the "Vietnam syndrome," the fear of the electoral effect of returning body bags, that led him to rule out ground operations in Kosovo, and to keep the planes on bombing missions above 15,000 feet so they would take no risks. The military stopped Wesley Clark from using Apache helicopters—in case they were shot at.

In Haiti, a mob of disgruntled Ton-Ton Macoute types on the quayside led the USS *Harlan County* to steam away humiliated with the U.S. and Canadian troops who were supposed to restore order. Despite an assured victory, even a minimal risk of casualties was unacceptable.

Already by November, the Iraq war had killed more Americans than the first three years of the Vietnam War. So why was public reaction to the increasing death rate in Iraq been so muted? Well one reason is that the public are not seeing body bags returning any more. Those body bags had already been euphemized into "transfer tubes" and, for once, following the good advice of his father who had instituted this policy in the first Gulf War, there were no cameras or grieving relatives allowed into Dover Air Force Base in Delaware, where the dead were brought back. There the Vietnam syndrome was known as the "Dover factor," the political effects of returning dead.

It has been said that you can measure a civilization by the way it treats its dead. And in many ways, modern America lavishes more attention on the deceased than the living, especially the military. In Europe, the tradition was to bury those killed in battle at or near where they met their dooms.

During the Civil War, the Union forces began a tradition of returning the dead to their homes and families and, to facilitate the process employed thousands of embalmers to preserve the departed. After the war, the flood of demobilized embalmers, full of Yankee entrepreneurial drive, transformed the funeral customs of the nation. No more "ashes to ashes, dust to dust." That American military tradition continues. Teams are still at work in Vietnam and Korea looking for the remains of fallen soldiers.

The bodies brought to Dover, packed in ice, are met with an honor guard that accompanies them to the new $30 million mortuary where they are embalmed, possible cosmetically restored, and dressed in full uniform for going home, along with a flag draped on the coffin. In a macabre technological touch, the military provides a bugler to play "Taps"—but has been running out of competent buglers so has introduced a sort of bugle-shaped music box that plays it electronically.

Neither the commander in chief, nor any of his entourage have attended any military funerals caused by the war he started. The White House line is that he wants to respect their privacy, and in March 2003, followed in the footsteps his father should have hidden better, the administration repeated and reinforced the policy that Bush the Elder had introduced in the first Gulf War. "There will be no arrival ceremonies for, or media coverage of, deceased military personnel returning to or departing from Ramstein (in Germany) or Dover base, to include interim stops."

As with the wounded at Walter Reed, the administration disguises the real reason it will not now allow the media to photograph or video the cortege from the plane, saying officially that it is to "to protect the wishes and privacy of the soldiers' families." But no one asked the families.

Most of the media have gone along with the administration policy, with honorable exceptions like *Newsday*, which published the photos and brief profiles of five American soldiers killed in Iraq in 2003, commenting bitterly, "Obscure people dying in obscurity." And, "The Pekinese of the press do not feel dead soldiers are worth mentioning. Only the guy next to them knew what they were made of."

Of course, what the policy ensures is that each funeral takes place with local media coverage, and avoids the amplifier effect of national newspaper and broadcast images of "wholesale" deaths at Dover Air Force base. The local media tell the harrowing stories of bereaved families and limn out the pictures of the dead. But those stories only rarely reach national attention.

Ironically, Bush has nothing against big funeral services. As governor of Texas he was closely involved in covering up for the world's biggest embalmers and funeral home chain, Service Corporation International, trying to ensure that they were protected from the Texas regulatory body that was investigating their practices. SCI were major donors for his campaigns—out of the profits from families that wanted serious ceremonies to say good-bye to their dead.

Wesley Clark has denounced the Bush policy, saying, "Our president has refused to attend a single funeral for a single soldier killed in Iraq. Even worse, he's banned media coverage and proper public ceremonies for deceased soldiers returning from the war—the kind of cover-up tactics we saw during Vietnam."

In April the truth bubbled to the surface like lava from under a volcano—explosively. Tami Silicio, a contract worker for Maytag in Kuwait wanted to show that the dead were being respectfully treated, and sent photographs of a plane hold filled with neatly aligned flag-draped coffins to the *Seattle Times*. She was fired, and gratuitously, so was her husband. The firm confessed to strong Pentagon pressure.

But her exposure was almost overshadowed by the Freedom of Information Act request of Russ Kick, the operator of a website, *The Memory Hole*. Almost to his surprise, his request for official DoD pictures was granted. Instead of a manageable stream of pictures, the administration was suddenly confronted with a wholesale rush of images of holds filled with dead, of the regular march from the planes to the mortuary.

The White House's protestations about the privacy of the families looked even more hollow than usual. These anonymous images showed the cost of war. And how could you invade a family's privacy more than taking one of their "loved ones," in the president's unctuous phrase, to the other side of the world and getting them killed.

Sometimes, sentimental concern for the dead conceals callousness to the living. Bush the Younger is consistent. Not only has he tried to hide and lessen the effect of the butcher's bill for his Iraqi adventure—he had showed what he thought of the survivors when in 2003 he tried to thwart the proposal to double the death grant. We could almost admire the consistency, if it were not that 2004 being election year, he has expediently dropped his opposition to the proposal—but redoubled his efforts to hide the human cost of the war.

This is perhaps a fitting place to lay this book to rest. Having spent a political lifetime burying his own efforts to ensure that he himself never risked arriving in a body bag at Dover, the self-styled commander in chief is now trying to make unknown soldiers of all those his obsessions have sent to die on foreign fields.

25 IF HE WERE NOT SERIOUS, HE WOULD BE A JOKE

WAS GEORGE W. BUSH A DESERTER? Possibly in the legal sense, but certainly in the moral sense. He took active and multiple steps to avoid physical risk in a war to which he lent political support—"the war of his generation." Absent without leave? Certainly. He went missing, failed to report for duty, and defied a direct order to attend a medical examination. In doing so he made himself unfit for his duty, flying, every bit as surely as if he had "let off a shotgun next to his ear." A careless child of privilege? Indisputably. He could not have done any of the above if he had not been armed with a silver spoon in his mouth. And while he has tried to hide that silver spoon with his folksy Texanisms, it is still there, even though it is surely not the reason he cannot pronounce nuclear, preferring the local "nucular."

But whatever dialect the affluent Ivy Leaguer now affects, above all he is a hypocrite, a poseur, and someone with dangerous daydreams of military might and prowess that may have been tempered if he had actually experienced combat first hand, or even had the empathy to feel for those who do. Would someone who had actually been in combat, crouched in a foxhole under enemy fire, or who had carried away the bleeding corpse of a dead comrade tell Iraqi insurgents "Bring 'em on"?

Long on arrogance, short on experience and empathy, the president of the United States has led this country and the world into a frightening twenty-first century. The old Latin question, *Quis custodiet ipsos custodies?*—"who polices the police"—has extra resonance when the world's only superpower is headed by a global scofflaw. We do not seriously expect terrorists to obey the law: if they did, they would not be terrorists! We expect governments and international institutions to try force them to. And we expect governments and international institutions to stick to the law when doing so. This president has been as cavalier with international law as he was with state law in Yale when stealing wreaths or driving under the influence.

Under the GOP's three strikes and you're out rule, a ghetto kid who stole a wreath could end up on behind bars for life and even if it was a first offense would have been unlikely to be launched on a political career path. Indeed a conviction in Florida would have made him unable to vote in the last election!

However, instead of the humility of an elected leader, we have a president who told Bob Woodward, "I'm the commander—see, I don't need to explain—I do not need to explain why I say things. That's the interesting thing about being the president. Maybe somebody needs to explain to me why they say something, but I don't feel like I owe anybody an explanation."53

In his April 13 press conference, the low point of an already low overall performance was when he was asked to identify mistakes he had made. Revealingly, the question pole-axed him. Inspired as he is by the Almighty, how could he make mistakes? What kind of heresy was this?

George W. Bush does not think that rules apply to him, and he thinks that they do not apply to his country, either. An era of hypocrisy and unbridled arbitrary power, domestically and internationally, is not the legacy that either the U.S. military—who are already paying the price—nor American citizens—who will be—should really want from the new millennium.

In this breathtakingly smug arrogance, we can see coming together all the traits we discussed earlier: the sense of privilege for being born rich, the sense of exaltation that God has chosen him to be rich, and the sense of almost sexual thrill from being commander in chief—and the complete and arrogant lack of any sense of accountability that this compounded privilege has given him.

General Wesley Clark said, "Republicans like weapons systems, Democrats like soldiers." Of course, some of the Democrats in office can be quite fond of the campaign contributions of weapons producers as well, but, in terms of the broad demographics, he probably has a point. In his autobiography in 1990 Bush declared, "Not since the days before

Pearl Harbor has our investment in national defense been so low a percentage of our gross national product. Nearly twelve thousand members of the armed forces are on food stamps. I support increased pay and better benefits and training for our citizen solders. A volunteer military has only two paths. It can lower its standards to fill its ranks. Or it can inspire the best and brightest to join and stay."[54]

As one would expect, this has at least two examples of what a British parliamentarian—constrained by the rules from calling lies—termed instead "terminological inexactitudes." While in 1941, the U.S. faced the potential threats from Germany, Japan, and Italy, when Bush wrote this the U.S. had no state enemy that could pose a significant military threat. And as we saw twenty-five thousand military families still need the food stamps but are now exposed to death and mutilation in a war whose causes are even murkier than the fabricated Tonkin Gulf incident used for Vietnam. At the end of April 2000, twenty thousand of them were ordered to stay beyond their twelve month tour "on the ground" in Iraq.

While it took some years for the falsity of the Tonkin Gulf incident to emerge, the evidence of mistaken strategies and contrived excuses by the Bush administration came flooding out almost immediately. And the evidence all points in the same direction. The disasters of the last few years, from September 11 to the invasion of Iraq and the uprising there a year later, were not only predictable: they were *predicted*, and the White House ignored the advice and disregarded the predictions.

The September 11 commission has revealed that there were numerous signals that something like the attack on the World Trade Center was in the offing. In 2001, the August 6 CIA Presidential Daily Briefing warned of hijackings, it warned that buildings in New York were under terrorist surveillance, it warned that something big was happening soon.

But the administration, headed by George W. Bush was, it seems, already planning a war on Iraq, and was too busy with that to get the signals. The reaction of Rumsfeld to September 11th was to ask for a bigger budget—not for intelligence or human resources to consolidate the information flow, but for more money for the "Star Wars" Strategic Defense Initiative, which, if less publicly and less spectacularly, has been almost as much an obsession as Saddam Hussein with him and the neocons. Rumsfeld's official bio notes prominently that under him the department "also has refocused its space capabilities and fashioned a new concept of strategic deterrence that increases security while reducing strategic nuclear weapons. To help strengthen the deterrent, the missile defense research and testing program has been reorganized and revitalized, free of the restraints of the ABM treaty." That's what he was working on while al-Qaeda prepared their attack in hijacked airliners against which his Star Wars systems offered no defense.

Before September 11, Democrats in the Senate tried to cut an administration request for a 57 percent increase in funding for missile defense and to divert $1.3 billion of the administration's request to, among other things, combating terrorism. In the wake of the World Trade Center collapse, all such attempts

at restraint were abandoned. On September 19 Senator Joe
Biden wrote:

> One of the lessons we should have learned from
> the devastating attack of September 11 is that ter-
> rorists determined to do this nation harm can
> employ a wide variety of means, and that weapons
> of mass destruction—chemical, biological or even
> nuclear—need not arrive on the tip of an inter-
> continental ballistic missile with a return address.
> That's why the Joint Chiefs of Staff argue that an
> ICBM launch ranks last on the "Threat Spec-
> trum," while terrorist attacks constitute the
> greatest potential threat to our national security.
>
> The administration's obsession with missile
> defense—with a price tag in excess of a quarter-
> trillion dollars for the layered program on the
> president's wish list—is doubly troubling because
> of the attention and resources being diverted from
> critical efforts to address genuine threats.

So on the one side, the administration's obsession with
orbiting hardware and aerospace industry dollars blinded
them to the realities of the threats facing the country, and on
the other side, the obsession with Iraq also meant that when
September 11 happened, the White House was totally unpre-
pared. But what is worse is that more and more evidence suggested that when it did happen, George W. Bush and his
advisers saw it almost as an opportunity as much as a tragedy.

It gave the cover they needed to advance their longstanding agenda against Saddam Hussein and Iraq.

This may seem almost libelous—but how else can a reasonable person interpret the very tangible facts? Osama bin Laden, the perpetrator in chief of the attack on the World Trade Center, is still at large in Afghanistan or its borders, with a handful of American troops engaged in the search. Saddam Hussein, against whom not the tiniest scintilla of evidence has been presented to connect him to September 11 is locked up, and almost the entire combat ready force of the U.S. has been tied up in Iraq, sending home body bags by the score a year after the flying popinjay announced "mission accomplished" on the decks of the USS *Abraham Lincoln*.

The outcome of the invasion of Iraq was, once again, predicable—and once again predicted. The State Department had foreseen the looting, the perils of dissolving the army and the government apparatus, and the likelihood of unrest. But no, the Pentagon, backed by the commander in chief, knew best. Which is why this is the first war where there have already been 400 percent more American dead *after* the war, as there were during—and in keeping with modern American media practices, we will not even begin to count the number of dead Iraqis who have paid the ultimate price for their liberation. At the very least, as a cynical French general once remarked, "It is worse than a crime—it is a blunder!"

There are heartening aspects to this. The un-American adulation of all that is military, cultivated so assiduously by the Republicans, is inherently unsound to advance the image of a George W. Bush. Although many in the military had scant time for Bill Clinton, at least he did not pass himself as some reinvented combat-hardened veteran, nor did he embroil them in a bloody and essentially unwinnable and misguided war in a faraway country. In these circumstances, for George W. Bush to posture as commander in chief and to belittle and disparage the military experience of his opponents, from John McCain to Wesley Clark to John Kerry, is a dangerous tactic.

If that is an effective line of attack for the Bush campaign, then it reinforces the validity of a Democratic counterattack on the absolute lack of a military record—and indeed on the more sinister *absence* of his military records from Alabama. It allows his opponents to point to the all-too-real record of Bush's war in Iraq: the wrong enemy, attacked the wrong way, with the wrong strategy. At the same time, the opponents of the war have learned their lesson, certainly as compared with Vietnam. It has taken a long time, but they now see the people in uniform as victims of an administration that has too many ideological cares to care much about the troops they are prepared to squander. Ironically, while he was maintaining low levels of pay and benefits for serving troops, Bush attacked Kerry for voting against the $87 billion that he asked Congress to appropriate for Iraq.

The attacks in Falluja showed the absurdities of Republican pork-barreling and privatization when applied to the military. It showed that Halliburton and the other private companies that had their snouts in the trough, had to make up for the shortfall in military manpower by hiring private security guards, who were being paid anything up to ten times the daily rate of their uniformed peers. And of course, they recruited experienced men from the military.

It used to be said that war was too important to be left to the generals. This almost proves that it is too important to be left to governments, at least this one.

In fact, the White House is under the control of fundamentalists, who close their eyes to any fact that does not harmonize with their preconceived ideas. They have recklessly exposed both the civilian population and the military to danger, because they were blind to the real dangers while they chased WMD windmills around the world.

As we have seen, the commander in chief prefers to talk at military bases rather than to civilians or the media. Soldiers are disciplined and keep their grouses inside. But in what was only his third press conference, because even the relatively anodyne U.S. press corps is feisty in comparison with the polite military, he revealed the core of his strategy to a reporter who made the comparison with Vietnam. "I . . . happen to think that analogy sends the wrong message to our troops, and sends the wrong message to the enemy." In short, anyone who criticizes the Bush administration policy is betraying our troops, and supporting the enemy.

The time is long past for us to rip off George W. Bush's feigned military splendor, to stop him wrapping himself in the flag—before any more of those flags are used to cover the remains of dismembered and shattered real soldiers. Too many people have died already to exorcise whatever demons haunt the young Googen Bush from his failure to emulate his father's genuine heroism.

Americans have far too much respect for presidents. Their every inanity is parsed with complete seriousness by commentators and pundits. We have been too polite with George W. Bush. His every appearance as commander in chief should evoke hoots of derision. His every pronouncement on military matters should be sneered at and questioned, and he should be pilloried for his lack of concern for those maimed and for the families orphaned and bereft by his policies. It is time for him to be given extended leave, even if we cannot persuade him to go missing for this war, the way he did his last.

APPENDIX

The Yale transcript.

15. I swear (or affirm) that the foregoing statements have been read to me, that my statements have been currently recorded and are true in all respects and that I fully understand the conditions under which I am enlisting.

SIGNATURE OF WITNESS DONALD DEAN BARNHART SGT   **SIGNATURE OF APPLICANT** (First Name - Middle Name - Last Name)

"I certify that the following statements are correct to the best of my knowledge:

The recruiter explained in detail all items of my enlistment contract to include the coding used and I understand them completely. I have furnished my latest DD Form 214, "Report of Transfer or Discharge" for previous military service and/or current information regarding reserve status, if any. The enlistment contract records my true name, date of birth, residence, school, and home of record. I am not a conscientious objector. I have been counseled and provided information on financial problems as a result of marriage while serving in the lower airman grade of E-4 with less than 4 years total service or below. I am not under orders for induction and my current Selective Service Classification is __IX-A__. I accept enlistment in the ANG (ResAF) in the grade of __AB__. I understand that from this date, I incur a service obligation of six (6) years under USC 651."

17. OATH OF ENLISTMENT (For service in Regular or Reserve Component of the Armed Forces except National Guard or Air National Guard)

I, _____ (First Name - Middle Name - Last Name) do hereby acknowledge to have voluntarily enlisted under the conditions prescribed by law, this ___ day of _____ in the _____ for a period of ___ years unless sooner discharged by proper authority and I do solemnly swear (or affirm) that I will support and defend the Constitution of the United States against all enemies, foreign and domestic; that I will bear true faith and allegiance to the same; and that I will obey the orders of the President of the United States and the orders of the officers appointed over me, according to regulations, and the Uniform Code of Military Justice. So help me God.

SIGNATURE

18. OATH OF ENLISTMENT (For service in National Guard or Air National Guard)

I do hereby acknowledge to have voluntarily enlisted this __27th__ day of __MAY__, 19 __68__ in the (Army) (Air) National Guard of the State of __TEXAS__ and as a Reserve of the (Army) (Air Force) with membership in the (Army) (Air) National Guard of the United States) for a period of __6 years__ under the conditions prescribed by law, unless sooner discharged by proper authority.

I, __GEORGE WALKER BUSH__ (First Name - Middle Name - Last Name) do solemnly swear (or affirm) that I will support and defend the Constitution of the United States and of the State of __TEXAS__ against all enemies, foreign and domestic; that I will bear true faith and allegiance to them; and that I will obey the orders of the President of the United States and the Governor of __TEXAS__ and the orders of the officers appointed over me, according to law, regulations, and the Uniform Code of Military Justice. So help me God.

George Walker Bush

19. CONFIRMATION OF ENLISTMENT

The above oath was subscribed and duly sworn to before me this __27th__ day of __MAY__, 19 __68__. To the best of my judgment and belief, enlistee fulfills all legal requirements, and in enlisting this applicant, I have strictly observed the regulations governing such enlistment. The above oath, as filled in, was read to the enlistee prior to subscribing thereto.

TYPED NAME, GRADE/RANK, AND ORGANIZATION OF ENLISTING OFFICER   **SIGNATURE OF ENLISTING OFFICER**

WILLIE J HOOVER JR, Capt, 147th Cmbt Spt Sq

1968: George W. Bush certifies he understands all the terms of his enlistment "completely."

STATEMENT OF INTENT

I, GEORGE WALKER BUSH, UPON SUCCESSFUL COMPLETION OF PILOT TRAINING
PLAN TO RETURN TO MY UNIT AND FULFILL MY OBLIGATION TO THE UTMOST
OF MY ABILITY. I HAVE APPLIED FOR PILOT TRAINING WITH THE GOAL OF
MAKING FLYING A LIFETIME PURSUIT AND I BELIEVE I CAN BEST ACCOMPLISH
THIS TO MY OWN SATISFACTION BY SERVING AS A MEMBER OF THE AIR NATIONAL
GUARD AS LONG AS POSSIBLE.

George Walker Bush
GEORGE WALKER BUSH

1968: He declares a lifetime interest in flying.

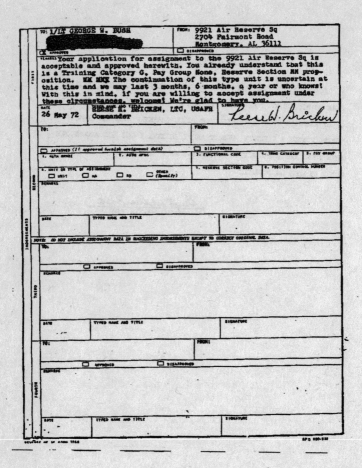

1972: His pals in the Texas ANG approve his transfer to a
"postal unit" in Alabama.

DESERTER 213

APPLICATION FOR RESERVE ASSIGNMENT

(This is a scanned military form, AF FORM 1288, "Application for Reserve Assignment")

TO: 9921st Air Reserve Squadron
c/o Lt. Col. Reese H. Bricken
2704 Fairmont — Montgomery, Ala. 36111

1. LAST NAME – FIRST NAME – MIDDLE INITIAL
Bush, George W.

2. DATE OF BIRTH
3. AFRES GRADE: 1/Lt.
4. DATE OF AFRES GRADE: Nov. 1970
7. PRIMARY AFSC: 1125B

9. CURRENT TERM OF APPOINTMENT OR ENLISTMENT: Sept., 1968

11. AERONAUTICAL RATING
Flying status

12. CIVILIAN EDUCATION
16 years
Yale University – 1968
BA – History

13. CIVILIAN EXPERIENCE
Red Blount For Senate – Campaign Management
Stratford of Texas – Assistant to Executive
Vice President – one year
George Bush For Senate – Surrogate Candidate

14. MILITARY SCHOOLS ATTENDED
none

15. MILITARY EXPERIENCE
Pilot, Fighter Interceptor
squadron level 1125B, 1/Lt.

16. PRESENT ASSIGNMENT AND ATTACHMENT
111th F.I.S. (TNG)
P. O. Box 34567
Houston, Texas 77034

17. ASSIGNMENT DESIRED
9921st Air Reserve Squadron
No pay, training category G
Reserve section MM

DATE: 24 May 72
SIGNATURE OF APPLICANT: George W. Bush

AF FORM 1288

Alabama National Guard says OK.

DEPARTMENT OF THE AIR FORCE
HEADQUARTERS AIR RESERVE PERSONNEL CENTER
3800 YORK STREET
DENVER, COLORADO 80205

REPLY TO
ATTN OF: DPMAA

SUBJECT: Application for Reserve Assignment, Bush, George W, 1st Lt, ████
USAFR

TO: TAG Texas

1. Application for Reserve Assignment for First Lieutenant Bush is
returned.

2. A review of his Master Personnel Record shows he has a Military
Service Obligation until 26 May 1974. Under the provisions of paragraph 30-6 a (4), AFM 35-3, an obligated Reservist can be assigned to
a specific Ready Reserve position only. Therefore, he is ineligible
for assignment to an Air Reserve Squadron.

FOR THE COMMANDER

[signature]

GWENT L. RALLIN, f.
Reserve Assignments Branch
Directorate of Personnel Resources

1 Atch
1. AF Fm 1288, 24 May 72 (2) w cash

Cy to: 1st Lt Bush
         147 Ftr Gp
         9921 Air Reserve Sq

1972: The Air Force cries foul and says he can't be transferred to
a non-active unit.

5th Ind to 1Lt George Bush Ltr, 5 Sep 72, Permission to Perform Equivalent Duty with 187th Tac Recon Gp

Hq. 187th Tac Recon Gp (DPM) 15 September 1972

TO: TAG, AL (AL-AFAB)

1. Approved. Unit Training Assembly schedule is as follows:

7-8 Oct 72   0730-1600
4-5 Nov 72   0730-1600
September UTA was held on 9-10 Sep 72.

2. Lieutenant Bush should report to LtCol William Turnipseed, DCO, to perform Equivalent Training. Lieutenant Bush will not be able to satisfy his flight requirements with our group.

FOR THE COMMANDER

KENNETH K. LOTT, Capt, AL ANG
Chief, Personnel Branch

6th Ind

TAG Alabama (AL-AFAB) 29 September 1972

TO: TAG Texas

Forwarded.

FOR THE ADJUTANT GENERAL

DAVID E. McCUTCHIN, 2d Lt, AL ANG   Cy to: Hq 117 TRW
Air Admin & Tng Off

7th Ind

TAG Texas, P O Box 5218, Austin, TX 78763 (AF) 21 Sep 72

TO: 147th Ftr Intcp Gp, TexANG

Forwarded.

FOR THE ADJUTANT GENERAL OF TEXAS

CHARLES K. SHOEMAN
Major, TexANG
Chief, Military Personnel Mgt

Bush is ordered to report to Lt Col. Turnipseed, who does not
remember him ever doing so.

AO 57, DAAF-AOA, dated 29 September 1972

CAPT BRIAN M LZIDING   Hq 182 Tac Air Spt Gp, Greater
           IL   Peoria Aprt, Peoria IL

CAPT EDWARD L SHARP   113 Tac Ftr Sq, Hulman Fld,
           IN   Terre Haute IN

CAPT WILBUR J LATHAM JR   124 Tac Ftr Sq, Des Moines MAP,
           IA   Des Moines IA

CAPT JAMES H RENSCHEN   103 Tac Air Spt Sq, Willow Grove NAS,
           PA   Willow Grove PA

4. Each of the fol named offs, ANGUS (Not on EAD), orgn indc, is
granted the aeronautical rating of Master Nav, per para 1-14d, AFM
35-13. Authority: Para 1-7b(5), AFM 35-13:

GRADE, NAME AND SSAN   ORGANIZATION

MAJ GENE J PESTY   136 Ftr Intcp Sq, Niagara Falls
           NY   Intl Aprt, Niagara Falls NY

LTCOL CARL R BECK   193 Tac Elect Warfare Sq, Olmsted
           PA   Fld, Middletown PA

5. CAPT DENNIS M HYATT, _____ ANGUS (Not on EAD), NY ANG,
136 Ftr Intcp Sq, Niagara Falls Intl Aprt, Niagara Falls NY, is
granted the aeronautical rating of Sen Nav per para 1-14e, AFM
35-13. Authority: Para 1-7b(5), AFM 35-13.

6. Verbal orders of the Comdr on 1 Aug 72 suspending 1STLT GEORGE W
BUSH, _____, ANGUS (Not on EAD), TX ANG, Hq 147 Ftr Gp, Ellington
AFB, Houston TX, from flying status are confirmed, exigencies of the
service having been such as to preclude the publication of competent
written orders in advance. Reason for Suspension: Failure to
accomplish annual medical examination. Off will comply with para
2-10, AFM 35-13. Authority: Para 2-29m, AFM 35-13.

7. Verbal orders of the Comdr on 1 Sep 72 suspending MAJ JAMES R BATH,
_____ ANGUS (Not on EAD), TX ANG, Hq 147 Ftr Gp, Ellington AFB,
Houston TX, from flying status are confirmed, exigencies of the service
having been such as to preclude the publication of competent written
orders in advance. Reason for Suspension: Failure to accomplish
annual medical examination. Off will comply with para 2-10, AFM 35-13.
Authority: Para 2-29m, AFM 35-13.

BY ORDER OF THE SECRETARIES OF THE ARMY AND THE AIR FORCE

                              FRANCIS S. GREENLIEF, Major General, USA
                              Chief, National Guard Bureau

OFFICIAL

GUIDO E. FINN, Colonel, USAF   DISTRIBUTION:
Executive, National Guard Bureau   15 ea State for ea Off
                                       1 AFMPC/DPMAJD
                                       1 NGB-AD
                                      25 NGB/DPM

1st Lt George W Bush is grounded for "failure to accomplish" annual
medical. The code means he is ordered to report and explain why he
didn't. He never does.

V. OVER-ALL EVAL

EFFECTIVE AND COMPETENT

PROMOTION POTENTIAL

VI.

VII.   COMMENTS

Lt Bush has not been observed at this unit during the period of report. A
civilian occupation made it necessary for him to move to Montgomery, Alabama.
He cleared this base on 15 May 1972 and has been performing equivalent training
in a non flying status with the 187 Tac Recon Gp, Dannelly AdG Base, Alabama.

VIII.   REPORTING OFFICIAL

WILLIAM D. HARRIS, JR. Lt Colonel
FG, 111th FIS
TxANG (AUC)

Pilot, Ftr Intcp

Command Pilot   1

2 May 1973   SIGNED

IX.   REVIEW BY INDORSING OFFICIAL

I concur with the comments of the reporting official.

JERRY B. KILLIAN, Lt Colonel
FG, 111th FIS
TxANG (AUC)

Squadron Commander

Command Pilot   1

2 May 1973   SIGNED

In May 1973, his best friends in Texas can find no excuses.
They have not seen him.

NOTICE OF MISSING OR ~~RREECTION~~ OF OFFICER EFFECTIVENESS ~~.~~ RAINING REPORT | DATE 2~ Jun 73 | SUSPENSE DATE 6 Aug 73

1	TO	INFO	FROM
	NGB/DPMO		ARPC/DPABB

LAST NAME · FIRST NAME · MIDDLE INITIAL	GRADE	SSAN	UNIT
BUSH, GEORGE W.	1Lt	▮▮▮▮	111 FISq

ATTACHED REPORT IS RETURNED FOR CORRECTION. REPORTING PERIOD | FROM 1 May 72 | THRU 30 Apr 73

CORRECTIVE ACTION REQUIRED AS INDICATED BELOW (Check applicable boxes)

1. A rating factor has not been checked in Item _____, Section _____.

2. A more comprehensive job description will be entered in Section II.

3. Rating factors in Section III, Items 1, 2, 3, 4, 5, 6, 7 and 8; Sections IV, V and VI do not agree on all copies.

4. OER will be reaccomplished due to erasure/correction in Section _____.

[X] 5. DAFSC and/or duty title in Section II does not agree with Item 8, AF Form 11.

6. Period of supervision incorrect.

7. Indorsing official must indicate his agreement/disagreement with ratings and comments of reporting official.

8. OER is returned for additional indorsement by an officer who meets the requirements of Rule _____, Table _____, AFM 36-10.

9. Required for indorsement by an officer in the grade of _____ or higher, as prescribed by AFM 36-10.

10. Reporting and/or indorsing official has not signed the report.

11. Period of report is incorrect, officer's last report closed on _____ therefore, this report must open _____.

12. OER must be in one complete original and one complete carbon copy.

13. Reporting and/or indorsing official has signed and closed the report prior to closing date.

[X] 14. Returned for compliance with paragraph 6-7f(3), AFM 36-10.

15. Request copy of Page 1 AF Form 11, IAF Para 4-1 f (2) AFM 36-10.

[X] 16. Returned for compliance with figure 6-25, AFM 36-10. _____ advised in regard to _____ official. Statement required by rule _____ Table _____, AFM 36-10.

17. _____

18. Other (Specify) [X] See Remarks

REMARKS (Reference item numbers)

Item 18. Ratings must be entered on this officer in Sections V & VI. An AF Fm 77a should be requested from the training unit so that this officer can be rated in the position he held. This officer should have been reassigned in May 1972 since he no longer is training in his AFSC or with his unit of assignment.

PLEASE RETURN ORIGINAL COPY OF THIS FORM WHEN RETURNING CORRECTED OER

TYPED NAME AND GRADE OF PERSONNEL OFFICER
DANIEL P. HARKNESS, MSgt, USAF
NCOIC, Selection Boards Branch | SIGNATURE _(signed)_

| 2 | TO TAC TEXAS | FROM NGB/DPMO | DATED 10 July | SUSPENSE ~~Aug~~ 73 |

REMARKS (If above suspense date cannot be met, furnish anticipated completion date.)

RETURN CORRECTED REPORT DIRECT TO ARPC

TYPED NAME AND GRADE OF PERSONNEL OFFICER | SIGNATURE Robert O'Neile

(When additional indorsements or remarks are required use reverse or blank sheets.)

ARPC FORM 204   *PREVIOUS EDITION DATED JUN 71 MAY BE USED.

Air Force reprimands Texas for not rating Bush. They dodge the issue until he has already left.

DEPARTMENT OF THE AIR FORCE
147TH FIGHTER INTERCEPTOR GROUP
ELLINGTON AIR FORCE BASE, TEXAS 77030

1 May 1973

SPECIAL ORDER
AE-226-TX

1. Fol named off and/or amn, orgns indicated, this station, are ordered to attend Annual Active Duty Training at the Air National Guard training site Ellington AFB, Texas for the period indicated: (Aero rating and fly status as indicated). Personnel will report to their unit commander for duty on effective date of training. Movement of dependents and household effects at government expense not authorized. Per diem and TPC authorized in accordance with JD 25-69 dated effective 9 July 1969. Rated personnel on flying status are authorized to participate in flying activities during the period covered by this order. Airmen within commuting distance (50mi.) are authorized basic allowances for subsistence at the rate of $2.57 per day (Per diem not payable) when rations in kind not available per paragraph 30102c DODPM. The bearer being the agent of an Air Force Reserve member on active duty in excess of 72 hours is authorized commissary privileges only for the period covered by these orders. Individuals not on active duty in excess of 72 hours are not authorized commissary privileges. P/A (Off) 5733850-563-4156-P521.01-6380000 (Amn) 5733850-563-4156-P521.07-6380000. Trans: (Off) 5733850-563-4145-P521.14-408-8414502 (Amn) 5733850-563-4145-P521.18-408-8414502. PD: (Off) 5733850-563-4145-P521.20-409-8414502 (Amn) 5733850-563-4145-P521.24-409-8414502. Authority: ANGM 50-01. Title 32, USC, Sec 503 (Formerly Sec 94, National Defense Act).

111TH FIGHTER INTERCEPTOR SQUADRON	NO DAYS	PERIOD
1ST LT GEORGE W. WUSH █████████	9	22May73 thru 24May73
AFSPC, 1125D Sqn ██████████		29May73 thru 31May73
		5Jun73 thru 7Jun73

2. SO AE 1 6 1 this Hqs, dated 13 Apr 73, pertaining to CAPT WAYNE K. WARE █████ only as reads "NO DAYS": 6. PERIOD: 18 Apr 73 thru 19 Apr █, 24 Apr █ thru 27 Apr 73 is amended to read "NO DAYS": 5. PERIOD: 18 to █ 73 thru 19 Apr 73, 24 Apr 73 thru 26 Apr 73.

FOR THE COMMANDER

BILLY B. LAMAR, CWO4 (USAF)
Asst Admin Officer

DISTRIBUTION
AE

AE-226-TX

Orders to Bush to turn up.

FROM: 111th Ftr Intcp Sq

SUBJECT: Application for Discharge   5 Sep 73

TO: 11Ith Ftr Intcp Sq/CC

I respectfully request my discharge from the Texas Air National Guard
and reassignment to ARPC (NARS) effective 1 October 1973. I am moving
to Boston, Massachusetts to attend Harvard Business School as a full time
student. I have enjoyed my association with the 111th Ftr Intcp Sq and
the 147th Ftr Intcp Gp.

[signature]

GEORGE W. BUSH, 1st Lt
▓▓▓▓▓▓▓ FC

1st Ind   6 Sep 73

111th Ftr Intcp Sq/CC

TO: 147th Ftr Intcp Gp/CC

Recommend approval.

[signature]

JERRY B. KILLIAN, Lt Col, TexANG
Commander

Bush drops out even further, applies to leave and be transferred
to a nominal reserve unit.

National Personnel Records Center

Military Personnel Records   9700 Page Avenue   St. Louis, Missouri 63132-5100

Martin E. Heldt
5101 2nd Ave. S
Clinton, IA 52732

Dear Mr. Heldt:

This is in response to your Freedom of Information Act request, dated December 22, 2003, seeking access to and copies of records or logs of any changes or additions made to the military records of George W. Bush, a former member of the United States Armed Forces.

The National Personnel Records Center has no records responsive to your request. Normally, any changes made to the records in our custody are made at the request of the veteran. There is a formal process to accomplish changes, and administrative boards have been created by each service branch to process requests for changes or corrections. Individual veterans, or their representatives, are required to use specific forms to request changes to their records. These forms are the DD Form 149, Application for Correction of Military Record under the Provisions of Title 10, U.S. Code, Section 1552, and DD Form 293, Application for the Review of Discharge or Dismissal from the Armed Forces of the United States. Copies of the application and the board action are filed with the Military Personnel Record after completion of all determinations. A complete review of Mr. Bush's records did not locate any requests for change, through use of the forms described above or by informal means, or any notification of changes made by the service department. The last action documented in the record was Mr. Bush's discharge from the Air Force Reserve on November 21, 1974. There are no entries in the record subsequent to that date.

It should be noted that tampering with or changing Federal records is a criminal offense under Title 18, Chapter 101, Section 2071, and is punishable by fine and or imprisonment.

This response does not constitute a denial of access under the provisions of the Freedom of Information Act.

Sincerely,

Charles Pellegrini
Chief, Management Systems Staff
National Personnel Records Center

Letter to Marty Heldt which suggests that Bush's service is actually extended by six months from May to November. Could this have been a disciplinary measure? Who knows?

WHITE HOUSE PRESS BRIEFING
FEBRUARY 13, 2004

Q (Helen Thomas): Did the president ever have to take time off from guard duty to do community service?

Scott McClellan: To do community service? I haven't looked into everything he did thirty years ago, Helen. Obviously, there is different community service he has performed in the past, including going back to that time period.

Q: Can you find out if he actually had—

Scott McClellan: Helen, I don't think we remember every single activity he was involved in thirty years ago.

Q: No, this isn't an activity. Was he forced to do community service at any time while he was on—

Scott McClellan: What's your interest in that question? I'm sorry, I just—

Q: Lots of rumors. I'm just trying to clear up something.

Scott McClellan: Rumors about what?

Q: Pardon?

Scott McClellan: Rumors about what?

Q: About the president having to do community service while he was in the National Guard, take time out for that.

Scott McClellan: I'm not aware of those rumors. But if you want to—

Q: Could you look it up? Would you mind asking him?

Scott McClellan: That's why I'm asking what's your interest in that? I just don't understand your interest in that.

Q: It's what everybody is interested in, whether we're getting the true story on his guard duty.

Scott McClellan: Well, you have the documents that show the facts.

Q: I'm asking you to try to find out from the president of the United States.

Scott McClellan: Like I said, it's well known the different jobs he had and what he was doing previously, that we know. That goes back to—

Q: I didn't say "previously." I said, while he was on guard duty.

Scott McClellan: But you're asking me about thirty years ago. I don't think there's a recollection of everything he was doing thirty years ago.

Q: Well, he would know if he had to take time out.

Scott McClellan: Again, I mean, the issue that was raised was whether or not the president was serving while he was in Alabama. Documents reflect that he was—

Q: Well, this is another issue.

Scott McClellan: —hold on—that he was serving in Alabama. That was the issue that was raised. We went through, four years ago, other issues related to this.

Q: So you won't answer the question or you won't try to find out?

Scott McClellan: Well, I'm asking you, what's your interest in that question? I'm just curious, because rumors—

Q: Did he have to do any community service while he was in the National Guard?

Scott McClellan: Look, Helen, I think the issue here was whether or not the president served in Alabama. Records have documented—

Q: I'm asking you a different question. That's permissible.

Scott McClellan: Can I answer your question? Sure it is. Can I ask you why you're asking it? I'm just—out of curiosity myself, is that permissible?

Q: Well, I'm interested, of course, in what everybody is interested in. And we have a very—

Scott McClellan: Let me just point out that we've released all the information we have related to this issue, the issue of whether or not he served while in Alabama. Records have documented as false the outrageous—

Q: I asked you whether he had to do any community service while he was in the National Guard.

Scott McClellan: Can I walk through this?

Q: It's a very legitimate question.

Scott McClellan: And I want to back up and walk through this a little bit. Let's talk about the issue that came up, because this issue came up four years ago, it came up four years before that—or two years before that, it came up four years before that—

Q: Did my question come up four years ago, and was it handled?

Scott McClellan: Helen, if you'll let me finish, I want to back up and talk about this—

Q: Don't dance around, just give us—

Q: It's a straightforward question.

Q: Let's not put too fine a point on it. If I'm not mistaken, you're implying that he had to do community service for criminal action, as a punishment for some crime?

Q: There are rumors around, and I didn't put it in that way. I just—

Q: Could you take that question? I guess apparently that's the question, that he had to take time out to perform community service—

Scott McClellan: That's why I wanted to get to this because—

Q: —as a sentence for a crime.

Scott McClellan: No, that's why I wanted to get to this because I want to step back for a second. I want to go back through a few things. Look, the—I think we've really exhausted the issue that came up. The issue that came up was related to whether or not he had served while he was in Alabama. Records have documented as false the outrageous, baseless accusation that he did not serve while in Alabama. The conspiracy theory of one individual, that the National Guard cleansed documents, has been discredited.

Q: How so?

Scott McClellan: Read the *Boston Globe* today.

Q: Well, we want answers from you, not—

Scott McClellan: Read the *Boston Globe*. No, the answers are from the people that would have knowledge of that. But read—

Q: Why do you think this person made those allegations?

Scott McClellan: Hang on, hang on.

Q: What? Just read the *Boston Globe*—

Scott McClellan: Just read the *Boston Globe*. Read the *Boston Globe*. I would draw your attention to that. What I think we're seeing now is just politics. And we're not going to engage in it, because there are great challenges facing our nation, and there should be an honest discussion of the actions the president is taking to make our world safer and better and make America more prosperous and secure. You want me to go—

Q: —the personal record of a president is—

Scott McClellan: No, hang on, Helen, hang on. I've said from this podium, if we have new information that comes to our attention that relates to this issue, we have made it clear we will share that information. You're asking me to go and chase rumors. There was a conspiracy theory—

Q: I think—

Scott McClellan: Hold on, hold on, Helen. There was a conspiracy theory made by one individual, when everybody he
accused of being involved in that said, it's ridiculous, didn't
happen.

Q: This is not based on a conspiracy theory.

Scott McClellan: And there was a lot of attention given to this
individual, and he's been discredited. There's a *Boston
Globe* article on it this morning. And there are some—

Q: That says what? Your point—

Scott McClellan: You can go read it. I mean, we've got other
things to move on to. I mean, you can go read it. But there
are some, unfortunately, who simply are not interested in
the facts. Again, the documents—the records document
that he did serve while in Alabama. And now there are
people that are bringing up issues that were addressed four
years ago.

Q: But you still haven't answered Helen's question. She asked
you a simple question.

Scott McClellan: There are people that want to replay the
2000 campaign all over again, Bill, and—

Q: You still haven't answered her question about community service.

Scott McClellan: —there are too many important—there are too many important policies and decisions that are being made that we need to discuss.

Q: Why does a "yes" or "no" elude you on this?

Scott McClellan: I didn't say that. I said that these were all issues addressed four years ago. If there's additional information—

Q: This issue quite obviously wasn't addressed four years ago.

Scott McClellan: Oh, issues—these issues were addressed four years ago.

Q: This issue was? The community service issue was addressed four years ago?

Scott McClellan: The issues—the issues that we're going to here—

Q: I don't recall—

Scott McClellan: This is called chasing a rumor. And I'm not going to engage in this kind of politics, Bill.

Q: —finding out whether a rumor is true or false.

Scott McClellan: No, this issue, absolutely—

Q: Why can't you say whether or not he performed community service?

Scott McClellan: Absolutely, this issue came up four years ago. And if you all want to play politics, then go call the RNC, call the campaign.

Q: The best defense is offense. We know that. Just, all you've got to say is you don't know.

Scott McClellan: Helen, it was—this issue was addressed four years ago. I think people that were involved in the campaign will know—

Q: —if they know—

Scott McClellan: —that the issue that you're trying to bring up was addressed four years ago. It's about chasing rumors.

Q: It isn't a question of four years ago. The issue has come up now, very large.

Scott McClellan: I'm not going to get into chasing rumors.

Q: Headlines.

Scott McClellan: I'm not going to get into chasing rumors.

Q: So you refuse to answer the question?

Scott McClellan: You're saying that people said he was forced to do something, and you're asking me to chase a rumor.

Q: Everything is politics today, of course.

Q: She asked you a "yes" or "no" question.

Scott McClellan: Look, if you all want to—this is just politics. That's what this is. And if there's any more information I have to share with you all, I will always—I will do that.

Q: Scott, I have a question of this individual, and I confess, I haven't read the Boston article. But who—what do you believe was this person's motivation, that if they have been discredited, for making these allegations?

Scott McClellan: Just—I would read the *Boston Globe*. Everybody that he accused of being involved in this has said it was totally ridiculous. And there are others that—

Q: So are you saying—was it politically motivated?

Scott McClellan: There are others that are quoted in the *Boston Globe* today, that you might want to see what they said.

Q: Speaking of politics, has the president authorized his campaign—

Scott McClellan: And we've got to—

Q: —to release a video attacking Senator Kerry?

Scott McClellan: You need to talk—you need to talk to the campaign. But let me go to the week ahead because we've used up more than fifteen minutes.

Q: So the president did authorize—

Q: Scott, I've got—

Scott McClellan: I'm going to go to the week ahead.

ENDNOTES

1. From the Greek *thamnos*, a "bush" or "shrub," like the Spanish, *arbusto*, it can mean "bush" or "shrub"

2. *Romanoff and Juliet*, Peter Ustinov
3. Elizabeth Bumiller, *New York Times*, May 2, 2002

4. Dave Lindorff, *In These Times*, December 22, 2003
5. Lee Hockstader, *Washington Post*, January 12, 2004

6. Dana Milbank, *Washington Post* staff writer, May 7, 2003

7. Robert Armstrong, in the Spycatcher trial NSW, 1986
8. *Charge to Keep*, George W. Bush and Karen Hughes. New York: Harper Collins, 1999. p. 50
9. *Charge to Keep*, p. 51
10. George Kuempel and Pete Slover, *The Dallas Morning News*, September 8, 1999.

11. *Fort Worth Star Telegram*, November 29, 1998
12. Colin Powell with Joseph Persico, *My American Journey*. New York: Random House, 1995, p.148
13. Walter V. Robinson, *Boston Globe*, July 28, 2000
14. *Charge to Keep*, p. 54
15. *Meet the Press*, February 8, 2004
16. *NPR Interview*, February 23, 2004
17. *Washington Post*, July 28, 1998. (See next)

18. *Charge to Keep*, p. 55

19. *Charge to Keep*, p. 6

20. *Bush at War*, Bob Woodward. New York: Simon and Schuster, 2002. p. 241

21. from the Journal of Human Relations, XVI 1968

22. *Charge to Keep*, p. 54

23. *Nightline*, February 12, 1992

24. September 24, 1776

25. Corelli Barnett *Britain and Her Army*, Allen Lane, 1970

26. Letter to Chandler Price, 1807

27. 1786 letter to James Munroe

28. Democratic vistas, 1870

29. George Lardner Jr. and Lois Romano, *At Height of Vietnam, Bush Picks Guard*, *Washington Post* staff

30. Chanda Temple, *Birmingham News*, October 14, 2000

31. Froomkin, *Washington Post*, February 3, 2004

32. Josh White, *Washington Post* staff writer, Sunday, February 22, 2004, p. A08

33. See *Sunday Times* (London), June 18, 2000

34. Salon Boehlert, February 17, 2004

35. Bush seen in Alabama in 1972, Jessica M. Walker, Gannett News Service

36. Jackson Baker, *Memphis Flyer*, February 13, 2004

37. Walter V. Robinson and Francie Latour, *Boston Globe*, February 12, 2004

38. Bush/Quayle Campaign Press Release, October 15, 1992

39. *Charge to Keep*, p. 55

40. *Texas Monthly*, June 1999

41. Gallup, February 16

42. Walter V. Robinson, *Boston Globe*, February 5, 2004

43. E. J. Dionne Jr., "Dirty Pool in Florida," *Washington Post*, Tuesday, July 17, 2001

44. *Business Week*, December 8, 2003

45. Woodward, p. 281

46. Karl Vick *Washington Post*, March 21, 2004

47. *Washington Post*, Jonathan Weisman, April 21, 2004

47. *Washington Post*, April 14, 2003

48. *Army Times*, June 30, 2003

49. Steve Vogel, *Washington Post*, October 21, 2003

50. Mark Benjamnin, UPI, April 1, 2004

51. Roosevelt Speech. Springfield (Illinois). July 4, 1903

52. Woodward, pp. 145, 156

53. *Charge to Keep*, p. 239

ACKNOWLEDGMENTS

This book would not have been possible without the previous work of outstanding journalists and other researchers and campaigners who would not take no for an answer, some of who were vilified and persecuted for their work. Some of them actively cooperated, and others did their bit simply by being published. They include in no particular order: Helen Thomas, Marty Heldt, Josh Marshall, Karen Kwiatkowski, Jeff Gold, Jill Greenberg, John Mason, Sheila Collins, Nick Mamatas, Marc Cooper, Eric Alterman, David Corn, Stuart Elliot, John Carlstrom, Molly Ivins, Michael Lindt, Glynn Wilson, Jake Tapper, Joe Conason, Bill Burkett, Bob Fertik, Trish Wood and Bobby Muller of Vietnam Veterans of America, Walter V. Robinson and Francie Latour, Susan Milligan of the *Boston Globe*, Wayne Slater, George Kuempl and Pete Slover of the *Dallas Morning News*, Dana Milbank, Lee Hockstader, George Lardner Jr., Dan Froomkin, Josh White, Lois Romano, Steve Vogel, Karl Vick of the *Washington Post*, Elizabeth Bumiller of the *New York Times*, James Ledbetter of *Time*, David Lindorff of *In These Times*, Ken Herman of the *Austin American-Statesman*, Chanda Temple of the *Birmingham News*, Tom Rhodes of the *Sunday Times* (London), Julian Borger of *The Guardian*, Eric Boehlert of *Salon*, Jackson Baker of the *Memphis Flyer*, Lou Dubose of *LA Weekly*, Mark Benjamin of *UPI*, Richard Serrano of the *LA Times*, Brett Blackledge, of the *Birmingham News*, Dave Moniz and Jim Drinkard of *USA Today*, Juan Gonzalez of *Newsday*, and the *Army Times*. They may not all agree with the use I've made of their work, but my thanks to them anyway!